# Lesson Plan and Record Book

## Table of Contents

This lesson plan book belongs to:

Name_____

School _____   School Year _____

Grade/Subject _____   Address _____

Room _____   Phone_____

*Teacher Created Materials, Inc.*
6421 Industry Way
Westminster, CA 92683
www.teachercreated.com

©*1999 Teacher Created Materials, Inc.*
Reprinted, 2002, a

Made in U.S.A.

**ISBN 1-57690-390-7**

**Editorial Project Manager**
Ina Massler Levin, M.A.

**Cover Art**
Sue Fullam and Chris Macabitas

**Editor**
Walter Kelly

**Imaging**
Ralph Olmedo, Jr.

# Ways to Use This Book

## Seating Charts (page 3–5)
Table or desk arrangement will vary depending on room size, grade level, and actual teaching style preferred. Six separate seating charts have been provided for your flexibility in the event you have different sections, change seating arrangements for different subjects, or elect to change seating arrangements periodically.

## Student Roster (pages 6 & 7)
Record both student and parent or guardian names and addresses. Make a special note of differences in last names when appropriate. You may wish to list siblings and their grades if they also attend your school. Notes may include special needs children and medications necessary.

## Substitute Teacher Information (pages 8 & 9)
Record all pertinent information on these pages. If you have a copy of the layout of your school, attach it to this page; otherwise, sketch an outline of the school grounds, showing restrooms, office, lounge, playground, etc. Paper clip this page as well as the lesson plan page for easy reference.

## Year at a Glance (page 10)
This section will give you an overview of the year and help focus on immediate and upcoming events, conferences, meetings, seminars, and other important dates. Record each event as soon as you are notified.

## Birthdays (page 11)
Write names and birthdates of students in boxes. Identify each special day with a birthday greeting. With young children, sing to them and present them with a special birthday hat.

## Emergency and First Aid Information (page 12)
Keep a first aid kit in an easy-to-find place and show the children where it is kept.

During the first week of school you may wish to go over the listed emergency information with your children.

In the blanks provided, list persons qualified to administer CPR along with their room numbers.

Literary Awards, Metric Conversions, Capital Cities, and World Map (pages 13–16)

These pages can be used as easy reference throughout the year. Also, you may wish to create puzzles and games using these fact pages.

## Class Record (pages 17–76)
The class record section is designed to provide organized space for recording daily notations or grades for assignments, tests, attendance, tardies, participation, etc. Each page contains a five-week block of spaces so that a student's record for an entire quarter of ten weeks can be read on facing pages. A summary column for recording total attendance, tardies, and grades appears on the right-hand facing page for each ten-week period. Enough record sheets are provided to last for two 20-week semesters, accomodating seven different classes or preparations. Two extra pages of record sheets covering 10 weeks (or one quarter) are provided for copy or replacement purposes.

## Daily Lesson Plans (pages 77–160)
Use the daily lesson plans section to help you organize your lesson plans for the week. In the blank that says "Week of____," add the dates for the week. You may wish to use the last column for notes or evaluation. Each weekly plan page has space to accomodate seven different subjects or sections, and there are enough pages to cover two 20-week semesters, including one extra.

Each weekly lesson plan features a proverb which can be used as a quote for the week. As sayings which have withstood the test of time, these proverbs are open to interpretation by the students. They can be shared by copying them onto the chalkboard, reading them aloud, using them to spark discussion and develop critical thinking skills, or assigning them as journal topics.

# Seating Charts

Class _____    Period _____

|  |  |  |  |  |  |  |
|---|---|---|---|---|---|---|
|  |  |  |  |  |  |  |
|  |  |  |  |  |  |  |
|  |  |  |  |  |  |  |
|  |  |  |  |  |  |  |
|  |  |  |  |  |  |  |
|  |  |  |  |  |  |  |

Class _____    Period _____

|  |  |  |  |  |  |  |
|---|---|---|---|---|---|---|
|  |  |  |  |  |  |  |
|  |  |  |  |  |  |  |
|  |  |  |  |  |  |  |
|  |  |  |  |  |  |  |
|  |  |  |  |  |  |  |
|  |  |  |  |  |  |  |

# Seating Charts *(cont.)*

Class _____  Period _____

| | | | | | | |
|---|---|---|---|---|---|---|
| | | | | | | |
| | | | | | | |
| | | | | | | |
| | | | | | | |
| | | | | | | |
| | | | | | | |
| | | | | | | |

Class _____  Period _____

| | | | | | | |
|---|---|---|---|---|---|---|
| | | | | | | |
| | | | | | | |
| | | | | | | |
| | | | | | | |
| | | | | | | |
| | | | | | | |
| | | | | | | |

# Seating Charts *(cont.)*

Class _____ Period _____

|  |  |  |  |  |  |  |
|---|---|---|---|---|---|---|
|  |  |  |  |  |  |  |
|  |  |  |  |  |  |  |
|  |  |  |  |  |  |  |
|  |  |  |  |  |  |  |
|  |  |  |  |  |  |  |
|  |  |  |  |  |  |  |

Class _____ Period _____

|  |  |  |  |  |  |  |
|---|---|---|---|---|---|---|
|  |  |  |  |  |  |  |
|  |  |  |  |  |  |  |
|  |  |  |  |  |  |  |
|  |  |  |  |  |  |  |
|  |  |  |  |  |  |  |
|  |  |  |  |  |  |  |

# Student Roster

| Name | Guardian | Telephone | Address |
|---|---|---|---|
| 1. | | | |
| 2. | | | |
| 3. | | | |
| 4. | | | |
| 5. | | | |
| 6. | | | |
| 7. | | | |
| 8. | | | |
| 9. | | | |
| 10. | | | |
| 11. | | | |
| 12. | | | |
| 13. | | | |
| 14. | | | |
| 15. | | | |
| 16. | | | |
| 17. | | | |
| 18. | | | |

# Student Roster *(cont.)*

| Name | Guardian | Telephone | Address |
|------|----------|-----------|---------|
| 19. | | | |
| 20. | | | |
| 21. | | | |
| 22. | | | |
| 23. | | | |
| 24. | | | |
| 25. | | | |
| 26. | | | |
| 27. | | | |
| 28. | | | |
| 29. | | | |
| 30. | | | |
| 31. | | | |
| 32. | | | |
| 33. | | | |
| 34. | | | |
| 35. | | | |
| 36. | | | |

# Substitute Teacher Information

## School Schedule
- Class Begins_____
- Morning Recess_____
- Lunchtime _____
- Class Resumes_____
- Afternoon Recess_____
- Dismissal _____

## Special Notes
_____
_____
_____
_____
_____
_____
_____
_____

## Special Classes
- Student _____

  Class _____ Day _____ Time _____
- Student _____

  Class _____ Day _____ Time _____
- Student _____

  Class _____ Day _____ Time _____

## Where to Find
- Class List _____
- School Layout _____
- Seating Chart _____
- Attendance Record_____
- Lesson Plans _____
- Teacher Manuals _____
- First Aid Kit _____
- Emergency Information _____
- Supplementary Activities _____
- Class Supplies—paper, pencils, etc _____
- Referral forms and procedures _____
_____
_____
_____
_____
_____
_____
_____
_____
_____
_____
_____
_____

## Special Needs Students

| Student | Needs | Time and Place |
| --- | --- | --- |
| _____ | _____ | _____ |
| _____ | _____ | _____ |
| _____ | _____ | _____ |
| _____ | _____ | _____ |
| _____ | _____ | _____ |
| _____ | _____ | _____ |
| _____ | _____ | _____ |

# Substitute Teacher Information *(cont.)*

## Classroom Standards

- When finished with an assignment

  _____

  _____

- When and how to speak out in class

  _____

  _____

- Incentive Program

  _____

  _____

- Discipline

  _____

  _____

- Restroom Procedure

  _____

  _____

## People Who Can Help

- Teacher/Room _____

- Dependable Students _____

  _____

  _____

  _____

  _____

  _____

- Principal _____

- Secretary _____

- Custodian _____

- Counselor _____

- Nurse _____

## Layout of School—including school office, teachers' lounge, restrooms, auditorium, playground, etc. (or attach printed diagram here)

# Year at a Glance

| August | September | October |
|---|---|---|
| | | |

| November | December | January |
|---|---|---|
| | | |

| February | March | April |
|---|---|---|
| | | |

| May | June | July |
|---|---|---|
| | | |

# Birthdays

| August | September | October |
|--------|-----------|---------|
| _____ | _____ | _____ |
| _____ | _____ | _____ |
| _____ | _____ | _____ |
| _____ | _____ | _____ |
| _____ | _____ | _____ |

| November | December | January |
|----------|----------|---------|
| _____ | _____ | _____ |
| _____ | _____ | _____ |
| _____ | _____ | _____ |
| _____ | _____ | _____ |

| February | March | April |
|----------|-------|-------|
| _____ | _____ | _____ |
| _____ | _____ | _____ |
| _____ | _____ | _____ |
| _____ | _____ | _____ |

| May | June | July |
|-----|------|------|
| _____ | _____ | _____ |
| _____ | _____ | _____ |
| _____ | _____ | _____ |

# Emergency and First Aid Information

## Classroom Caution

- Do not move a person who is seriously injured.
- Report all head injuries to the nurse or office.
- Show children where the first aid kit is stored.
- List students with medical problems and any medications.
- Instruct children about nose blowing and covering their mouths when coughing and sneezing.
- Inform students about what to do if they feel they are going to be ill.
- The best way to stop bleeding is to put pressure on the wound.

  a. Use a clean pad, a cloth, a plastic bag, or any other object that will keep you from touching the blood directly. (Never allow the blood to touch your skin.)

  b. Place your hand over the pad or cloth, pressing firmly and steadily until the bleeding stops or someone comes to help.

  c. Do not remove the pad or cloth. You might start the bleeding again. Instead, add more pads or cloth and keep pressing.

  d. If the part that is bleeding can be raised higher than the victim's head, do so; this will slow down the flow of blood.

  e. Keep the victim from moving—especially the wounded area.

## First Aid for Choking
### Adults/Children

**If conscious but *choking*...**

Give abdominal thrusts until object comes out.

**If person becomes *unconscious*...**

**Step 1**
Clear any object from the mouth.

**Step 2**
Give two slow breaths.

**If air won't go in...**

**Step 3**
Give up to five abdominal thrusts.

**Repeat** steps 1, 2, & 3 until breaths go in or help arrives.

## Trained CPR person at our school:

Name _____ Room _____

Name _____ Room _____

Name _____ Room _____

Name _____ Room _____

Name _____ Room _____

Name _____ Room _____

Name _____ Room _____

# Newbery and Caldecott Awards

**The Newbery Medal** is awarded each year to the author of the most distinguished contribution to children's literature published in the United States. Here are the winners from 1960 to 2000.

**The Caldecott Medal** is presented to the illustrator of the most distinguished picture book for children published in the United States. Here are the winners from 1960 to 2000.

### Year Title/Author

2000 *Bud, Not Buddy.* Christopher Paul Curtis
1999 *Holes.* Louis Sachar
1998 *Out of The Dust.* Karen Hesse
1997 *The View from Saturday.* E.L. Konigsburg
1996 *Midwife's Apprentice.* Karen Cushman
1995 *Walk Two Moons.* Sharon Creech
1994 *The Giver.* Lois Lowry
1993 *Missing May.* Cynthia Rylant
1992 *Shiloh.* Phyllis Reynolds
1991 *Maniac Magee.* Jerry Spinelli
1990 *Number the Stars.* Lois Lowry
1989 *Joyful Noise.* Paul Fleischman
1988 *Lincoln: A Photobiography.* Russell Freedman
1987 *The Whipping Boy.* Sid Fleischman
1986 *Sarah, Plain and Tall.* Patricia MacLachlan
1985 *The Hero and the Crown.* Robin McKinley
1984 *Dear Mr. Henshaw.* Beverly Cleary
1983 *Dicey's Song.* Cynthia Voigt
1982 *A Visit to William Blake's Inn.* Nancy Willard
1981 *Jacob Have I Loved.* Katherine Paterson
1980 *A Gathering of Days.* Joan W. Blos
1979 *The Westing Game.* Ellen Raskin
1978 *Bridge to Terabithia.* Katherine Paterson
1977 *Roll of Thunder, Hear My Cry.* Mildred Taylor
1976 *The Grey King.* Susan Cooper
1975 *M.C. Higgins, the Great.* Virginia Hamilton
1974 *The Slave Dancer.* Paula Fox
1973 *Julie of the Wolves.* Jean George
1972 *Mrs. Frisby and the Rats of NIMH.* Robert C. O'Brien
1971 *Summer of the Swans.* Betsy Byars
1970 *Sounder.* William H. Armstrong
1969 *The High King.* Lloyd Alexander
1968 *From the Mixed-Up Files of Mrs. Basil E. Frankweiler.* E.L. Konigsburg
1967 *Up a Road Slowly.* Irene Hunt
1966 *I, Juan de Pareja.* Elizabeth Borton de Trevino
1965 *Shadow of a Bull.* Maia Wojciechowska
1964 *It's Like This, Cat.* Emily C. Neville
1963 *A Wrinkle in Time.* Madeline L'Engle
1962 *The Bronze Bow.* Elizabeth C. Speare
1961 *Island of the Blue Dolphins.* Scott O'Dell
1960 *Onion John.* Joseph Krumgold

### Year Title/Illustrator

2000 *Joseph Had a Little Overcoat.* Simms Tabak
1999 *Snowflake Bentley.* Jacqueline Briggs Martin
1998 *Rapunzel.* Paul O. Zelinsky
1997 *Golem.* David Wishiewski
1996 *Officer Buckle and Gloria.* P. Rathmann
1995 *Smoky Night.* David Diaz.
1994 *Grandfather's Journey.* Allen Say
1993 *Mirette on the High Wire.* Emily A. McCully
1992 *Tuesday.* David Wiesner
1991 *Black and White.* David Macauley
1990 *Lon Po Po.* Ed Young
1989 *Song and Dance Man.* Stephen Gammell
1988 *Owl Moon.* John Schoenherr
1987 *Hey, Al.* Richard Egielski
1986 *The Polar Express.* Chris Van Allsburg
1985 *Saint George and the Dragon.* Trina Schart Hyman
1984 *The Glorious Flight: Across the Channel with Louis Bleriot.* Alice and Martin Provensen
1983 *Shadow.* Marcia Brown
1982 *Jumanji.* Chris Van Allsburg
1981 *Fables.* Arnold Lobel
1980 *Ox-Cart Man.* Barbara Cooney
1979 *The Girl Who Loved Wild Horses.* Paul Goble
1978 *Noah's Ark.* Peter Spier
1977 *Ashanti to Zulu: African Traditions.* Leo and Diane Dillon
1976 *Why Mosquitoes Buzz in People's Ears.* Leo and Diane Dillon
1975 *Arrow to the Sun: A Pueblo Indian Tale.* Gerald Mc Dermott
1974 *Duffy and the Devil.* Margot Zemach
1973 *The Funny Little Woman.* Blair Lent
1972 *One Fine Day.* Nonny Hogrogian
1971 *A Story, A Story.* Gail E. Haley
1970 *Sylvester and the Magic Pebble.* William Steig
1969 *The Fool of the World and the Flying Ship.* Uri Shulevitz
1968 *Drummer Hoff.* Ed Emberly
1967 *Sam, Bangs and Moonshine.* Evaline Ness
1966 *Always Room for One More.* Nonny Hogrogian
1965 *May I Bring a Friend?* Beni Montresor
1964 *Where the Wild Things Are.* Maurice Sendak
1963 *The Snowy Day.* Ezra Jack Keats
1962 *Once a Mouse.* Marcia Brown
1961 *Baboushka and the Three Kings.* Nicholas Sidjakov
1960 *Nine Days to Christmas.* Marie Hall Ets

# Metric Conversions

## Linear

| | | |
|---|---|---|
| 100 cm | = | 1 meter |
| cm | = | centimeter |
| ¼" | = | .64 cm |
| ½" | = | 1.3 cm |
| 1" | = | 2.54 cm |
| 3" | = | 7.62 cm |
| 6" | = | 15.24 cm |
| 9" | = | 22.86 cm |
| 12" | = | 30.48 cm |
| 18" | = | 45.72 cm |
| 24" | = | 61 cm |
| 36" | = | 91.44 cm |
| 100 yds | = | 91.4 m |
| 1 mile | = | 1,609 m |

## Volume (dry and liquid)

| | | |
|---|---|---|
| L | = | liter |
| mL | = | milliliter = .001 L |
| 1 tsp | = | 5 mL |
| 1 T | = | 15 mL |
| ¼ c | = | 59 mL |
| ½ c | = | 118 mL |
| 1 c | = | 236 mL or 8 oz. = .236 L |
| 1 oz | = | 30 mL |
| 1 pt | = | about .5 L (473.2 mL) |
| 1 qt | = | about 1 L (946.3 mL) |
| 1 gal | = | about 3.8 L |
| 1 L | = | 1.0567 qts liquid |
| 1 qt dry | = | 1.101 L |
| 1 qt liquid | = | 0.9463 L |
| 1 gal liquid | = | 3.78541 L |

## Temperatures

To convert Fahrenheit to Celsius (F° - 32 x .55)
To convert Celsius to Fahrenheit (C° x 1.8) + 32

| | Celsius | Fahrenheit |
|---|---|---|
| boiling point of water . . . . . . | 100° | 212° |
| freezing point of water . . . . . | 0° | 32° |
| cold day . . . . . . . . . . . . . . . | -20° | -4° |
| room temperature . . . . . . . . | 20° | 66° |
| body temperature . . . . . . . . | 37° | 98.6° |

### Oven Temperatures

| | Celsius | Fahrenheit |
|---|---|---|
| warm oven . . . . . . . . . . . . . | 135° | 275° |
| moderate oven . . . . . . . . . . | 175° | 350° |
| hot oven . . . . . . . . . . . . . . . | 204° | 400° |

## Weights

| | | |
|---|---|---|
| 1 gram | = | 0.03527 ounce |
| 1 ounce | = | 28.35 grams |
| 1 kilogram | = | 2.2046 lbs |
| 1 pound | = | 453.4 grams or .454 kilogram |
| 1 ton | = | 908 kilograms |

# States, Provinces and Capitals

## UNITED STATES

| State | Capital |
|---|---|
| Alabama | Montgomery |
| Alaska | Juneau |
| Arizona | Phoenix |
| Arkansas | Little Rock |
| California | Sacramento |
| Colorado | Denver |
| Connecticut | Hartford |
| Delaware | Dover |
| Florida | Tallahassee |
| Georgia | Atlanta |
| Hawaii | Honolulu |
| Idaho | Boise |
| Illinois | Springfield |
| Indiana | Indianapolis |
| Iowa | Des Moines |
| Kansas | Topeka |
| Kentucky | Frankfort |
| Louisiana | Baton Rouge |
| Maine | Augusta |
| Maryland | Annapolis |
| Massachusetts | Boston |
| Michigan | Lansing |
| Minnesota | St. Paul |
| Mississippi | Jackson |
| Missouri | Jefferson City |
| Montana | Helena |
| Nebraska | Lincoln |
| Nevada | Carson City |
| New Hampshire | Concord |
| New Jersey | Trenton |
| New Mexico | Santa Fe |
| New York | Albany |
| North Carolina | Raleigh |
| North Dakota | Bismarck |
| Ohio | Columbus |
| Oklahoma | Oklahoma City |
| Oregon | Salem |
| Pennsylvania | Harrisburg |
| Rhode Island | Providence |
| South Carolina | Columbia |
| South Dakota | Pierre |
| Tennessee | Nashville |
| Texas | Austin |
| Utah | Salt Lake City |
| Vermont | Montpelier |
| Virginia | Richmond |
| Washington | Olympia |
| West Virginia | Charleston |
| Wisconsin | Madison |
| Wyoming | Cheyenne |
| Nation's Capital | Washington, D.C. |

## CANADA

| Province | Capital |
|---|---|
| Alberta | Edmonton |
| British Columbia | Victoria |
| Manitoba | Winnipeg |
| New Brunswick | Fredericton |
| Newfoundland | St. John's |
| Nova Scotia | Halifax |
| Ontario | Toronto |
| Prince Edward Island | Charlottetown |
| Quebec | Quebec |
| Saskatchewan | Regina |

**Territories**

| | |
|---|---|
| Northwest Territories | Yellowknife |
| Yukon Territory | Whitehorse |

## MEXICO

| State | Capital |
|---|---|
| Aguascalientes | Aguascalientes |
| Baja California Norte | Mexicali |
| Baja California Sur | La Paz |
| Campeche | Campeche |
| Chiapas | Tuxtla Gutierrez |
| Chihuahua | Chihuahua |
| Coahuila | Saltillo |
| Colima | Colima |
| Durango | Durango |
| Federal District | — |
| Guanajuato | Guanajuato |
| Guerrero | Chilpancingo |
| Hidalgo | Pachuca |
| Jalisco | Guadalajara |
| México | Toluca |
| Michoacán | Morelia |
| Morelos | Cuernavaca |
| Nayarit | Tepic |
| Nuevo León | Monterrey |
| Oaxaca | Oaxaca |
| Puebla | Puebla |
| Querétaro | Querétaro |
| Quintana Roo | Chetumal |
| San Luis Potosí | San Luis Potosí |
| Sinaloa | Culiacán |
| Sonora | Hermosillo |
| Tabasco | Villahermosa |
| Tamaulipas | Ciudad Victoria |
| Tlaxcala | Tlaxcala |
| Veracruz | Jalapa |
| Yucatán | Mérida |
| Zacatecas | Zacatecas |

# World Map

3000 Km
3000 Mi.
Scale at the Equator

# Class Record Section

# Subject_____

| Week | Week____ | | | | Week____ | | | | Week____ | | | | Week____ | | | | Week____ | | | |
|---|---|---|---|---|---|---|---|---|---|---|---|---|---|---|---|---|---|---|---|---|
| Day | M | T | W | T | F | M | T | W | T | F | M | T | W | T | F | M | T | W | T | F | M | T | W | T | F |
| Date | | | | | | | | | | | | | | | | | | | | | | | | | |
| Assignments or Attendance | | | | | | | | | | | | | | | | | | | | | | | | | |
| Name | | | | | | | | | | | | | | | | | | | | | | | | | |
| 1 | | | | | | | | | | | | | | | | | | | | | | | | | |
| 2 | | | | | | | | | | | | | | | | | | | | | | | | | |
| 3 | | | | | | | | | | | | | | | | | | | | | | | | | |
| 4 | | | | | | | | | | | | | | | | | | | | | | | | | |
| 5 | | | | | | | | | | | | | | | | | | | | | | | | | |
| 6 | | | | | | | | | | | | | | | | | | | | | | | | | |
| 7 | | | | | | | | | | | | | | | | | | | | | | | | | |
| 8 | | | | | | | | | | | | | | | | | | | | | | | | | |
| 9 | | | | | | | | | | | | | | | | | | | | | | | | | |
| 10 | | | | | | | | | | | | | | | | | | | | | | | | | |
| 11 | | | | | | | | | | | | | | | | | | | | | | | | | |
| 12 | | | | | | | | | | | | | | | | | | | | | | | | | |
| 13 | | | | | | | | | | | | | | | | | | | | | | | | | |
| 14 | | | | | | | | | | | | | | | | | | | | | | | | | |
| 15 | | | | | | | | | | | | | | | | | | | | | | | | | |
| 16 | | | | | | | | | | | | | | | | | | | | | | | | | |
| 17 | | | | | | | | | | | | | | | | | | | | | | | | | |
| 18 | | | | | | | | | | | | | | | | | | | | | | | | | |
| 19 | | | | | | | | | | | | | | | | | | | | | | | | | |
| 20 | | | | | | | | | | | | | | | | | | | | | | | | | |
| 21 | | | | | | | | | | | | | | | | | | | | | | | | | |
| 22 | | | | | | | | | | | | | | | | | | | | | | | | | |
| 23 | | | | | | | | | | | | | | | | | | | | | | | | | |
| 24 | | | | | | | | | | | | | | | | | | | | | | | | | |
| 25 | | | | | | | | | | | | | | | | | | | | | | | | | |
| 26 | | | | | | | | | | | | | | | | | | | | | | | | | |
| 27 | | | | | | | | | | | | | | | | | | | | | | | | | |
| 28 | | | | | | | | | | | | | | | | | | | | | | | | | |
| 29 | | | | | | | | | | | | | | | | | | | | | | | | | |
| 30 | | | | | | | | | | | | | | | | | | | | | | | | | |
| 31 | | | | | | | | | | | | | | | | | | | | | | | | | |
| 32 | | | | | | | | | | | | | | | | | | | | | | | | | |
| 33 | | | | | | | | | | | | | | | | | | | | | | | | | |
| 34 | | | | | | | | | | | | | | | | | | | | | | | | | |
| 35 | | | | | | | | | | | | | | | | | | | | | | | | | |
| 36 | | | | | | | | | | | | | | | | | | | | | | | | | |

# Period_____

| Week____ | | | | | Week____ | | | | | Week____ | | | | | Week____ | | | | | Week____ | | | | | | Days Present | Days Absent | Tardies | Quarter Grade | |
|---|---|---|---|---|---|---|---|---|---|---|---|---|---|---|---|---|---|---|---|---|---|---|---|---|---|---|---|---|---|---|
| M | T | W | T | F | M | T | W | T | F | M | T | W | T | F | M | T | W | T | F | M | T | W | T | F | | | | | | |
| | | | | | | | | | | | | | | | | | | | | | | | | | 1 | | | | | |
| | | | | | | | | | | | | | | | | | | | | | | | | | 2 | | | | | |
| | | | | | | | | | | | | | | | | | | | | | | | | | 3 | | | | | |
| | | | | | | | | | | | | | | | | | | | | | | | | | 4 | | | | | |
| | | | | | | | | | | | | | | | | | | | | | | | | | 5 | | | | | |
| | | | | | | | | | | | | | | | | | | | | | | | | | 6 | | | | | |
| | | | | | | | | | | | | | | | | | | | | | | | | | 7 | | | | | |
| | | | | | | | | | | | | | | | | | | | | | | | | | 8 | | | | | |
| | | | | | | | | | | | | | | | | | | | | | | | | | 9 | | | | | |
| | | | | | | | | | | | | | | | | | | | | | | | | | 10 | | | | | |
| | | | | | | | | | | | | | | | | | | | | | | | | | 11 | | | | | |
| | | | | | | | | | | | | | | | | | | | | | | | | | 12 | | | | | |
| | | | | | | | | | | | | | | | | | | | | | | | | | 13 | | | | | |
| | | | | | | | | | | | | | | | | | | | | | | | | | 14 | | | | | |
| | | | | | | | | | | | | | | | | | | | | | | | | | 15 | | | | | |
| | | | | | | | | | | | | | | | | | | | | | | | | | 16 | | | | | |
| | | | | | | | | | | | | | | | | | | | | | | | | | 17 | | | | | |
| | | | | | | | | | | | | | | | | | | | | | | | | | 18 | | | | | |
| | | | | | | | | | | | | | | | | | | | | | | | | | 19 | | | | | |
| | | | | | | | | | | | | | | | | | | | | | | | | | 20 | | | | | |
| | | | | | | | | | | | | | | | | | | | | | | | | | 21 | | | | | |
| | | | | | | | | | | | | | | | | | | | | | | | | | 22 | | | | | |
| | | | | | | | | | | | | | | | | | | | | | | | | | 23 | | | | | |
| | | | | | | | | | | | | | | | | | | | | | | | | | 24 | | | | | |
| | | | | | | | | | | | | | | | | | | | | | | | | | 25 | | | | | |
| | | | | | | | | | | | | | | | | | | | | | | | | | 26 | | | | | |
| | | | | | | | | | | | | | | | | | | | | | | | | | 27 | | | | | |
| | | | | | | | | | | | | | | | | | | | | | | | | | 28 | | | | | |
| | | | | | | | | | | | | | | | | | | | | | | | | | 29 | | | | | |
| | | | | | | | | | | | | | | | | | | | | | | | | | 30 | | | | | |
| | | | | | | | | | | | | | | | | | | | | | | | | | 31 | | | | | |
| | | | | | | | | | | | | | | | | | | | | | | | | | 32 | | | | | |
| | | | | | | | | | | | | | | | | | | | | | | | | | 33 | | | | | |
| | | | | | | | | | | | | | | | | | | | | | | | | | 34 | | | | | |
| | | | | | | | | | | | | | | | | | | | | | | | | | 35 | | | | | |
| | | | | | | | | | | | | | | | | | | | | | | | | | 36 | | | | | |

# Subject_____

| Week | Week____ | | | | | Week____ | | | | | Week____ | | | | | Week____ | | | | | Week____ | | | | |
|---|---|---|---|---|---|---|---|---|---|---|---|---|---|---|---|---|---|---|---|---|---|---|---|---|---|
| Day | M | T | W | T | F | M | T | W | T | F | M | T | W | T | F | M | T | W | T | F | M | T | W | T | F |
| Date | | | | | | | | | | | | | | | | | | | | | | | | | |
| Assignments or Attendance | | | | | | | | | | | | | | | | | | | | | | | | | |
| Name | | | | | | | | | | | | | | | | | | | | | | | | | |
| 1 | | | | | | | | | | | | | | | | | | | | | | | | | |
| 2 | | | | | | | | | | | | | | | | | | | | | | | | | |
| 3 | | | | | | | | | | | | | | | | | | | | | | | | | |
| 4 | | | | | | | | | | | | | | | | | | | | | | | | | |
| 5 | | | | | | | | | | | | | | | | | | | | | | | | | |
| 6 | | | | | | | | | | | | | | | | | | | | | | | | | |
| 7 | | | | | | | | | | | | | | | | | | | | | | | | | |
| 8 | | | | | | | | | | | | | | | | | | | | | | | | | |
| 9 | | | | | | | | | | | | | | | | | | | | | | | | | |
| 10 | | | | | | | | | | | | | | | | | | | | | | | | | |
| 11 | | | | | | | | | | | | | | | | | | | | | | | | | |
| 12 | | | | | | | | | | | | | | | | | | | | | | | | | |
| 13 | | | | | | | | | | | | | | | | | | | | | | | | | |
| 14 | | | | | | | | | | | | | | | | | | | | | | | | | |
| 15 | | | | | | | | | | | | | | | | | | | | | | | | | |
| 16 | | | | | | | | | | | | | | | | | | | | | | | | | |
| 17 | | | | | | | | | | | | | | | | | | | | | | | | | |
| 18 | | | | | | | | | | | | | | | | | | | | | | | | | |
| 19 | | | | | | | | | | | | | | | | | | | | | | | | | |
| 20 | | | | | | | | | | | | | | | | | | | | | | | | | |
| 21 | | | | | | | | | | | | | | | | | | | | | | | | | |
| 22 | | | | | | | | | | | | | | | | | | | | | | | | | |
| 23 | | | | | | | | | | | | | | | | | | | | | | | | | |
| 24 | | | | | | | | | | | | | | | | | | | | | | | | | |
| 25 | | | | | | | | | | | | | | | | | | | | | | | | | |
| 26 | | | | | | | | | | | | | | | | | | | | | | | | | |
| 27 | | | | | | | | | | | | | | | | | | | | | | | | | |
| 28 | | | | | | | | | | | | | | | | | | | | | | | | | |
| 29 | | | | | | | | | | | | | | | | | | | | | | | | | |
| 30 | | | | | | | | | | | | | | | | | | | | | | | | | |
| 31 | | | | | | | | | | | | | | | | | | | | | | | | | |
| 32 | | | | | | | | | | | | | | | | | | | | | | | | | |
| 33 | | | | | | | | | | | | | | | | | | | | | | | | | |
| 34 | | | | | | | | | | | | | | | | | | | | | | | | | |
| 35 | | | | | | | | | | | | | | | | | | | | | | | | | |
| 36 | | | | | | | | | | | | | | | | | | | | | | | | | |

# Period

| Week____ | | | | | Week____ | | | | | Week____ | | | | | Week____ | | | | | Week____ | | | | | | Days Present | Days Absent | Tardies | Quarter Grade | |
|---|---|---|---|---|---|---|---|---|---|---|---|---|---|---|---|---|---|---|---|---|---|---|---|---|---|---|---|---|---|---|
| M | T | W | T | F | M | T | W | T | F | M | T | W | T | F | M | T | W | T | F | M | T | W | T | F | | | | | | |
| | | | | | | | | | | | | | | | | | | | | | | | | | 1 | | | | | |
| | | | | | | | | | | | | | | | | | | | | | | | | | 2 | | | | | |
| | | | | | | | | | | | | | | | | | | | | | | | | | 3 | | | | | |
| | | | | | | | | | | | | | | | | | | | | | | | | | 4 | | | | | |
| | | | | | | | | | | | | | | | | | | | | | | | | | 5 | | | | | |
| | | | | | | | | | | | | | | | | | | | | | | | | | 6 | | | | | |
| | | | | | | | | | | | | | | | | | | | | | | | | | 7 | | | | | |
| | | | | | | | | | | | | | | | | | | | | | | | | | 8 | | | | | |
| | | | | | | | | | | | | | | | | | | | | | | | | | 9 | | | | | |
| | | | | | | | | | | | | | | | | | | | | | | | | | 10 | | | | | |
| | | | | | | | | | | | | | | | | | | | | | | | | | 11 | | | | | |
| | | | | | | | | | | | | | | | | | | | | | | | | | 12 | | | | | |
| | | | | | | | | | | | | | | | | | | | | | | | | | 13 | | | | | |
| | | | | | | | | | | | | | | | | | | | | | | | | | 14 | | | | | |
| | | | | | | | | | | | | | | | | | | | | | | | | | 15 | | | | | |
| | | | | | | | | | | | | | | | | | | | | | | | | | 16 | | | | | |
| | | | | | | | | | | | | | | | | | | | | | | | | | 17 | | | | | |
| | | | | | | | | | | | | | | | | | | | | | | | | | 18 | | | | | |
| | | | | | | | | | | | | | | | | | | | | | | | | | 19 | | | | | |
| | | | | | | | | | | | | | | | | | | | | | | | | | 20 | | | | | |
| | | | | | | | | | | | | | | | | | | | | | | | | | 21 | | | | | |
| | | | | | | | | | | | | | | | | | | | | | | | | | 22 | | | | | |
| | | | | | | | | | | | | | | | | | | | | | | | | | 23 | | | | | |
| | | | | | | | | | | | | | | | | | | | | | | | | | 24 | | | | | |
| | | | | | | | | | | | | | | | | | | | | | | | | | 25 | | | | | |
| | | | | | | | | | | | | | | | | | | | | | | | | | 26 | | | | | |
| | | | | | | | | | | | | | | | | | | | | | | | | | 27 | | | | | |
| | | | | | | | | | | | | | | | | | | | | | | | | | 28 | | | | | |
| | | | | | | | | | | | | | | | | | | | | | | | | | 29 | | | | | |
| | | | | | | | | | | | | | | | | | | | | | | | | | 30 | | | | | |
| | | | | | | | | | | | | | | | | | | | | | | | | | 31 | | | | | |
| | | | | | | | | | | | | | | | | | | | | | | | | | 32 | | | | | |
| | | | | | | | | | | | | | | | | | | | | | | | | | 33 | | | | | |
| | | | | | | | | | | | | | | | | | | | | | | | | | 34 | | | | | |
| | | | | | | | | | | | | | | | | | | | | | | | | | 35 | | | | | |
| | | | | | | | | | | | | | | | | | | | | | | | | | 36 | | | | | |

© Teacher Created Materials, Inc.

#2390 Lesson Plan and Record Book

# Subject_____

| Week | Week____ | | | | | Week____ | | | | | Week____ | | | | | Week____ | | | | | Week____ | | | | |
|---|---|---|---|---|---|---|---|---|---|---|---|---|---|---|---|---|---|---|---|---|---|---|---|---|---|
| Day | M | T | W | T | F | M | T | W | T | F | M | T | W | T | F | M | T | W | T | F | M | T | W | T | F |
| Date | | | | | | | | | | | | | | | | | | | | | | | | | |
| Assignments or Attendance | | | | | | | | | | | | | | | | | | | | | | | | | |
| Name | | | | | | | | | | | | | | | | | | | | | | | | | |
| 1 | | | | | | | | | | | | | | | | | | | | | | | | | |
| 2 | | | | | | | | | | | | | | | | | | | | | | | | | |
| 3 | | | | | | | | | | | | | | | | | | | | | | | | | |
| 4 | | | | | | | | | | | | | | | | | | | | | | | | | |
| 5 | | | | | | | | | | | | | | | | | | | | | | | | | |
| 6 | | | | | | | | | | | | | | | | | | | | | | | | | |
| 7 | | | | | | | | | | | | | | | | | | | | | | | | | |
| 8 | | | | | | | | | | | | | | | | | | | | | | | | | |
| 9 | | | | | | | | | | | | | | | | | | | | | | | | | |
| 10 | | | | | | | | | | | | | | | | | | | | | | | | | |
| 11 | | | | | | | | | | | | | | | | | | | | | | | | | |
| 12 | | | | | | | | | | | | | | | | | | | | | | | | | |
| 13 | | | | | | | | | | | | | | | | | | | | | | | | | |
| 14 | | | | | | | | | | | | | | | | | | | | | | | | | |
| 15 | | | | | | | | | | | | | | | | | | | | | | | | | |
| 16 | | | | | | | | | | | | | | | | | | | | | | | | | |
| 17 | | | | | | | | | | | | | | | | | | | | | | | | | |
| 18 | | | | | | | | | | | | | | | | | | | | | | | | | |
| 19 | | | | | | | | | | | | | | | | | | | | | | | | | |
| 20 | | | | | | | | | | | | | | | | | | | | | | | | | |
| 21 | | | | | | | | | | | | | | | | | | | | | | | | | |
| 22 | | | | | | | | | | | | | | | | | | | | | | | | | |
| 23 | | | | | | | | | | | | | | | | | | | | | | | | | |
| 24 | | | | | | | | | | | | | | | | | | | | | | | | | |
| 25 | | | | | | | | | | | | | | | | | | | | | | | | | |
| 26 | | | | | | | | | | | | | | | | | | | | | | | | | |
| 27 | | | | | | | | | | | | | | | | | | | | | | | | | |
| 28 | | | | | | | | | | | | | | | | | | | | | | | | | |
| 29 | | | | | | | | | | | | | | | | | | | | | | | | | |
| 30 | | | | | | | | | | | | | | | | | | | | | | | | | |
| 31 | | | | | | | | | | | | | | | | | | | | | | | | | |
| 32 | | | | | | | | | | | | | | | | | | | | | | | | | |
| 33 | | | | | | | | | | | | | | | | | | | | | | | | | |
| 34 | | | | | | | | | | | | | | | | | | | | | | | | | |
| 35 | | | | | | | | | | | | | | | | | | | | | | | | | |
| 36 | | | | | | | | | | | | | | | | | | | | | | | | | |

# Period_____

| Week____ | | | | | Week____ | | | | | Week____ | | | | | Week____ | | | | | Week____ | | | | | | Days Present | Days Absent | Tardies | Quarter Grade | |
|---|---|---|---|---|---|---|---|---|---|---|---|---|---|---|---|---|---|---|---|---|---|---|---|---|---|---|---|---|---|---|
| M | T | W | T | F | M | T | W | T | F | M | T | W | T | F | M | T | W | T | F | M | T | W | T | F | | | | | | |
| | | | | | | | | | | | | | | | | | | | | | | | | | 1 | | | | | |
| | | | | | | | | | | | | | | | | | | | | | | | | | 2 | | | | | |
| | | | | | | | | | | | | | | | | | | | | | | | | | 3 | | | | | |
| | | | | | | | | | | | | | | | | | | | | | | | | | 4 | | | | | |
| | | | | | | | | | | | | | | | | | | | | | | | | | 5 | | | | | |
| | | | | | | | | | | | | | | | | | | | | | | | | | 6 | | | | | |
| | | | | | | | | | | | | | | | | | | | | | | | | | 7 | | | | | |
| | | | | | | | | | | | | | | | | | | | | | | | | | 8 | | | | | |
| | | | | | | | | | | | | | | | | | | | | | | | | | 9 | | | | | |
| | | | | | | | | | | | | | | | | | | | | | | | | | 10 | | | | | |
| | | | | | | | | | | | | | | | | | | | | | | | | | 11 | | | | | |
| | | | | | | | | | | | | | | | | | | | | | | | | | 12 | | | | | |
| | | | | | | | | | | | | | | | | | | | | | | | | | 13 | | | | | |
| | | | | | | | | | | | | | | | | | | | | | | | | | 14 | | | | | |
| | | | | | | | | | | | | | | | | | | | | | | | | | 15 | | | | | |
| | | | | | | | | | | | | | | | | | | | | | | | | | 16 | | | | | |
| | | | | | | | | | | | | | | | | | | | | | | | | | 17 | | | | | |
| | | | | | | | | | | | | | | | | | | | | | | | | | 18 | | | | | |
| | | | | | | | | | | | | | | | | | | | | | | | | | 19 | | | | | |
| | | | | | | | | | | | | | | | | | | | | | | | | | 20 | | | | | |
| | | | | | | | | | | | | | | | | | | | | | | | | | 21 | | | | | |
| | | | | | | | | | | | | | | | | | | | | | | | | | 22 | | | | | |
| | | | | | | | | | | | | | | | | | | | | | | | | | 23 | | | | | |
| | | | | | | | | | | | | | | | | | | | | | | | | | 24 | | | | | |
| | | | | | | | | | | | | | | | | | | | | | | | | | 25 | | | | | |
| | | | | | | | | | | | | | | | | | | | | | | | | | 26 | | | | | |
| | | | | | | | | | | | | | | | | | | | | | | | | | 27 | | | | | |
| | | | | | | | | | | | | | | | | | | | | | | | | | 28 | | | | | |
| | | | | | | | | | | | | | | | | | | | | | | | | | 29 | | | | | |
| | | | | | | | | | | | | | | | | | | | | | | | | | 30 | | | | | |
| | | | | | | | | | | | | | | | | | | | | | | | | | 31 | | | | | |
| | | | | | | | | | | | | | | | | | | | | | | | | | 32 | | | | | |
| | | | | | | | | | | | | | | | | | | | | | | | | | 33 | | | | | |
| | | | | | | | | | | | | | | | | | | | | | | | | | 34 | | | | | |
| | | | | | | | | | | | | | | | | | | | | | | | | | 35 | | | | | |
| | | | | | | | | | | | | | | | | | | | | | | | | | 36 | | | | | |

# Subject _____

| Week | Week____ | | | | | Week____ | | | | | Week____ | | | | | Week____ | | | | | Week____ | | | | | Week____ | | | |
|---|---|---|---|---|---|---|---|---|---|---|---|---|---|---|---|---|---|---|---|---|---|---|---|---|---|---|---|---|---|
| Day | M | T | W | T | F | M | T | W | T | F | M | T | W | T | F | M | T | W | T | F | M | T | W | T | F | M | T | W | T |
| Date | | | | | | | | | | | | | | | | | | | | | | | | | | | | | |
| Assignments or Attendance | | | | | | | | | | | | | | | | | | | | | | | | | | | | | |
| Name | | | | | | | | | | | | | | | | | | | | | | | | | | | | | |
| 1 | | | | | | | | | | | | | | | | | | | | | | | | | | | | | |
| 2 | | | | | | | | | | | | | | | | | | | | | | | | | | | | | |
| 3 | | | | | | | | | | | | | | | | | | | | | | | | | | | | | |
| 4 | | | | | | | | | | | | | | | | | | | | | | | | | | | | | |
| 5 | | | | | | | | | | | | | | | | | | | | | | | | | | | | | |
| 6 | | | | | | | | | | | | | | | | | | | | | | | | | | | | | |
| 7 | | | | | | | | | | | | | | | | | | | | | | | | | | | | | |
| 8 | | | | | | | | | | | | | | | | | | | | | | | | | | | | | |
| 9 | | | | | | | | | | | | | | | | | | | | | | | | | | | | | |
| 10 | | | | | | | | | | | | | | | | | | | | | | | | | | | | | |
| 11 | | | | | | | | | | | | | | | | | | | | | | | | | | | | | |
| 12 | | | | | | | | | | | | | | | | | | | | | | | | | | | | | |
| 13 | | | | | | | | | | | | | | | | | | | | | | | | | | | | | |
| 14 | | | | | | | | | | | | | | | | | | | | | | | | | | | | | |
| 15 | | | | | | | | | | | | | | | | | | | | | | | | | | | | | |
| 16 | | | | | | | | | | | | | | | | | | | | | | | | | | | | | |
| 17 | | | | | | | | | | | | | | | | | | | | | | | | | | | | | |
| 18 | | | | | | | | | | | | | | | | | | | | | | | | | | | | | |
| 19 | | | | | | | | | | | | | | | | | | | | | | | | | | | | | |
| 20 | | | | | | | | | | | | | | | | | | | | | | | | | | | | | |
| 21 | | | | | | | | | | | | | | | | | | | | | | | | | | | | | |
| 22 | | | | | | | | | | | | | | | | | | | | | | | | | | | | | |
| 23 | | | | | | | | | | | | | | | | | | | | | | | | | | | | | |
| 24 | | | | | | | | | | | | | | | | | | | | | | | | | | | | | |
| 25 | | | | | | | | | | | | | | | | | | | | | | | | | | | | | |
| 26 | | | | | | | | | | | | | | | | | | | | | | | | | | | | | |
| 27 | | | | | | | | | | | | | | | | | | | | | | | | | | | | | |
| 28 | | | | | | | | | | | | | | | | | | | | | | | | | | | | | |
| 29 | | | | | | | | | | | | | | | | | | | | | | | | | | | | | |
| 30 | | | | | | | | | | | | | | | | | | | | | | | | | | | | | |
| 31 | | | | | | | | | | | | | | | | | | | | | | | | | | | | | |
| 32 | | | | | | | | | | | | | | | | | | | | | | | | | | | | | |
| 33 | | | | | | | | | | | | | | | | | | | | | | | | | | | | | |
| 34 | | | | | | | | | | | | | | | | | | | | | | | | | | | | | |
| 35 | | | | | | | | | | | | | | | | | | | | | | | | | | | | | |
| 36 | | | | | | | | | | | | | | | | | | | | | | | | | | | | | |

# Period

| Week____ | | | | | Week____ | | | | | Week____ | | | | | Week____ | | | | | Week____ | | | | | | Days Present | Days Absent | Tardies | Quarter Grade | |
|---|---|---|---|---|---|---|---|---|---|---|---|---|---|---|---|---|---|---|---|---|---|---|---|---|---|---|---|---|---|---|
| M | T | W | T | F | M | T | W | T | F | M | T | W | T | F | M | T | W | T | F | M | T | W | T | F | | | | | | |
| | | | | | | | | | | | | | | | | | | | | | | | | | | | | | | |
| | | | | | | | | | | | | | | | | | | | | | | | | | 1 | | | | | |
| | | | | | | | | | | | | | | | | | | | | | | | | | 2 | | | | | |
| | | | | | | | | | | | | | | | | | | | | | | | | | 3 | | | | | |
| | | | | | | | | | | | | | | | | | | | | | | | | | 4 | | | | | |
| | | | | | | | | | | | | | | | | | | | | | | | | | 5 | | | | | |
| | | | | | | | | | | | | | | | | | | | | | | | | | 6 | | | | | |
| | | | | | | | | | | | | | | | | | | | | | | | | | 7 | | | | | |
| | | | | | | | | | | | | | | | | | | | | | | | | | 8 | | | | | |
| | | | | | | | | | | | | | | | | | | | | | | | | | 9 | | | | | |
| | | | | | | | | | | | | | | | | | | | | | | | | | 10 | | | | | |
| | | | | | | | | | | | | | | | | | | | | | | | | | 11 | | | | | |
| | | | | | | | | | | | | | | | | | | | | | | | | | 12 | | | | | |
| | | | | | | | | | | | | | | | | | | | | | | | | | 13 | | | | | |
| | | | | | | | | | | | | | | | | | | | | | | | | | 14 | | | | | |
| | | | | | | | | | | | | | | | | | | | | | | | | | 15 | | | | | |
| | | | | | | | | | | | | | | | | | | | | | | | | | 16 | | | | | |
| | | | | | | | | | | | | | | | | | | | | | | | | | 17 | | | | | |
| | | | | | | | | | | | | | | | | | | | | | | | | | 18 | | | | | |
| | | | | | | | | | | | | | | | | | | | | | | | | | 19 | | | | | |
| | | | | | | | | | | | | | | | | | | | | | | | | | 20 | | | | | |
| | | | | | | | | | | | | | | | | | | | | | | | | | 21 | | | | | |
| | | | | | | | | | | | | | | | | | | | | | | | | | 22 | | | | | |
| | | | | | | | | | | | | | | | | | | | | | | | | | 23 | | | | | |
| | | | | | | | | | | | | | | | | | | | | | | | | | 24 | | | | | |
| | | | | | | | | | | | | | | | | | | | | | | | | | 25 | | | | | |
| | | | | | | | | | | | | | | | | | | | | | | | | | 26 | | | | | |
| | | | | | | | | | | | | | | | | | | | | | | | | | 27 | | | | | |
| | | | | | | | | | | | | | | | | | | | | | | | | | 28 | | | | | |
| | | | | | | | | | | | | | | | | | | | | | | | | | 29 | | | | | |
| | | | | | | | | | | | | | | | | | | | | | | | | | 30 | | | | | |
| | | | | | | | | | | | | | | | | | | | | | | | | | 31 | | | | | |
| | | | | | | | | | | | | | | | | | | | | | | | | | 32 | | | | | |
| | | | | | | | | | | | | | | | | | | | | | | | | | 33 | | | | | |
| | | | | | | | | | | | | | | | | | | | | | | | | | 34 | | | | | |
| | | | | | | | | | | | | | | | | | | | | | | | | | 35 | | | | | |
| | | | | | | | | | | | | | | | | | | | | | | | | | 36 | | | | | |

#2390 Lesson Plan and Record Book

# Subject_____

| Week_____ | Week____ | | | | Week____ | | | | Week____ | | | | Week____ | | | | Week____ | | | | Week____ | | | |
|---|---|---|---|---|---|---|---|---|---|---|---|---|---|---|---|---|---|---|---|---|---|---|---|---|
| Day | M | T | W | T | F | M | T | W | T | F | M | T | W | T | F | M | T | W | T | F | M | T | W | T | F |
| Date | | | | | | | | | | | | | | | | | | | | | | | | | |
| Assignments or Attendance | | | | | | | | | | | | | | | | | | | | | | | | | |
| Name | | | | | | | | | | | | | | | | | | | | | | | | | |
| 1 | | | | | | | | | | | | | | | | | | | | | | | | | |
| 2 | | | | | | | | | | | | | | | | | | | | | | | | | |
| 3 | | | | | | | | | | | | | | | | | | | | | | | | | |
| 4 | | | | | | | | | | | | | | | | | | | | | | | | | |
| 5 | | | | | | | | | | | | | | | | | | | | | | | | | |
| 6 | | | | | | | | | | | | | | | | | | | | | | | | | |
| 7 | | | | | | | | | | | | | | | | | | | | | | | | | |
| 8 | | | | | | | | | | | | | | | | | | | | | | | | | |
| 9 | | | | | | | | | | | | | | | | | | | | | | | | | |
| 10 | | | | | | | | | | | | | | | | | | | | | | | | | |
| 11 | | | | | | | | | | | | | | | | | | | | | | | | | |
| 12 | | | | | | | | | | | | | | | | | | | | | | | | | |
| 13 | | | | | | | | | | | | | | | | | | | | | | | | | |
| 14 | | | | | | | | | | | | | | | | | | | | | | | | | |
| 15 | | | | | | | | | | | | | | | | | | | | | | | | | |
| 16 | | | | | | | | | | | | | | | | | | | | | | | | | |
| 17 | | | | | | | | | | | | | | | | | | | | | | | | | |
| 18 | | | | | | | | | | | | | | | | | | | | | | | | | |
| 19 | | | | | | | | | | | | | | | | | | | | | | | | | |
| 20 | | | | | | | | | | | | | | | | | | | | | | | | | |
| 21 | | | | | | | | | | | | | | | | | | | | | | | | | |
| 22 | | | | | | | | | | | | | | | | | | | | | | | | | |
| 23 | | | | | | | | | | | | | | | | | | | | | | | | | |
| 24 | | | | | | | | | | | | | | | | | | | | | | | | | |
| 25 | | | | | | | | | | | | | | | | | | | | | | | | | |
| 26 | | | | | | | | | | | | | | | | | | | | | | | | | |
| 27 | | | | | | | | | | | | | | | | | | | | | | | | | |
| 28 | | | | | | | | | | | | | | | | | | | | | | | | | |
| 29 | | | | | | | | | | | | | | | | | | | | | | | | | |
| 30 | | | | | | | | | | | | | | | | | | | | | | | | | |
| 31 | | | | | | | | | | | | | | | | | | | | | | | | | |
| 32 | | | | | | | | | | | | | | | | | | | | | | | | | |
| 33 | | | | | | | | | | | | | | | | | | | | | | | | | |
| 34 | | | | | | | | | | | | | | | | | | | | | | | | | |
| 35 | | | | | | | | | | | | | | | | | | | | | | | | | |
| 36 | | | | | | | | | | | | | | | | | | | | | | | | | |

# Period_____

| | Week____ | | | | Week____ | | | | Week____ | | | | Week____ | | | | Week____ | | | | | Days Present | Days Absent | Tardies | Quarter Grade | |
|---|---|---|---|---|---|---|---|---|---|---|---|---|---|---|---|---|---|---|---|---|---|---|---|---|---|---|---|
| M | T | W | T | F | M | T | W | T | F | M | T | W | T | F | M | T | W | T | F | M | T | W | T | F | | | | | | |
| | | | | | | | | | | | | | | | | | | | | | | | | | 1 | | | | | |
| | | | | | | | | | | | | | | | | | | | | | | | | | 2 | | | | | |
| | | | | | | | | | | | | | | | | | | | | | | | | | 3 | | | | | |
| | | | | | | | | | | | | | | | | | | | | | | | | | 4 | | | | | |
| | | | | | | | | | | | | | | | | | | | | | | | | | 5 | | | | | |
| | | | | | | | | | | | | | | | | | | | | | | | | | 6 | | | | | |
| | | | | | | | | | | | | | | | | | | | | | | | | | 7 | | | | | |
| | | | | | | | | | | | | | | | | | | | | | | | | | 8 | | | | | |
| | | | | | | | | | | | | | | | | | | | | | | | | | 9 | | | | | |
| | | | | | | | | | | | | | | | | | | | | | | | | | 10 | | | | | |
| | | | | | | | | | | | | | | | | | | | | | | | | | 11 | | | | | |
| | | | | | | | | | | | | | | | | | | | | | | | | | 12 | | | | | |
| | | | | | | | | | | | | | | | | | | | | | | | | | 13 | | | | | |
| | | | | | | | | | | | | | | | | | | | | | | | | | 14 | | | | | |
| | | | | | | | | | | | | | | | | | | | | | | | | | 15 | | | | | |
| | | | | | | | | | | | | | | | | | | | | | | | | | 16 | | | | | |
| | | | | | | | | | | | | | | | | | | | | | | | | | 17 | | | | | |
| | | | | | | | | | | | | | | | | | | | | | | | | | 18 | | | | | |
| | | | | | | | | | | | | | | | | | | | | | | | | | 19 | | | | | |
| | | | | | | | | | | | | | | | | | | | | | | | | | 20 | | | | | |
| | | | | | | | | | | | | | | | | | | | | | | | | | 21 | | | | | |
| | | | | | | | | | | | | | | | | | | | | | | | | | 22 | | | | | |
| | | | | | | | | | | | | | | | | | | | | | | | | | 23 | | | | | |
| | | | | | | | | | | | | | | | | | | | | | | | | | 24 | | | | | |
| | | | | | | | | | | | | | | | | | | | | | | | | | 25 | | | | | |
| | | | | | | | | | | | | | | | | | | | | | | | | | 26 | | | | | |
| | | | | | | | | | | | | | | | | | | | | | | | | | 27 | | | | | |
| | | | | | | | | | | | | | | | | | | | | | | | | | 28 | | | | | |
| | | | | | | | | | | | | | | | | | | | | | | | | | 29 | | | | | |
| | | | | | | | | | | | | | | | | | | | | | | | | | 30 | | | | | |
| | | | | | | | | | | | | | | | | | | | | | | | | | 31 | | | | | |
| | | | | | | | | | | | | | | | | | | | | | | | | | 32 | | | | | |
| | | | | | | | | | | | | | | | | | | | | | | | | | 33 | | | | | |
| | | | | | | | | | | | | | | | | | | | | | | | | | 34 | | | | | |
| | | | | | | | | | | | | | | | | | | | | | | | | | 35 | | | | | |
| | | | | | | | | | | | | | | | | | | | | | | | | | 36 | | | | | |

# Subject_____

| Week | Week____ | | | | | Week____ | | | | | Week____ | | | | | Week____ | | | | | Week____ | | | | |
|---|---|---|---|---|---|---|---|---|---|---|---|---|---|---|---|---|---|---|---|---|---|---|---|---|---|
| Day | M | T | W | T | F | M | T | W | T | F | M | T | W | T | F | M | T | W | T | F | M | T | W | T | F |
| Date | | | | | | | | | | | | | | | | | | | | | | | | | |
| Assignments or Attendance | | | | | | | | | | | | | | | | | | | | | | | | | |
| Name | | | | | | | | | | | | | | | | | | | | | | | | | |
| 1 | | | | | | | | | | | | | | | | | | | | | | | | | |
| 2 | | | | | | | | | | | | | | | | | | | | | | | | | |
| 3 | | | | | | | | | | | | | | | | | | | | | | | | | |
| 4 | | | | | | | | | | | | | | | | | | | | | | | | | |
| 5 | | | | | | | | | | | | | | | | | | | | | | | | | |
| 6 | | | | | | | | | | | | | | | | | | | | | | | | | |
| 7 | | | | | | | | | | | | | | | | | | | | | | | | | |
| 8 | | | | | | | | | | | | | | | | | | | | | | | | | |
| 9 | | | | | | | | | | | | | | | | | | | | | | | | | |
| 10 | | | | | | | | | | | | | | | | | | | | | | | | | |
| 11 | | | | | | | | | | | | | | | | | | | | | | | | | |
| 12 | | | | | | | | | | | | | | | | | | | | | | | | | |
| 13 | | | | | | | | | | | | | | | | | | | | | | | | | |
| 14 | | | | | | | | | | | | | | | | | | | | | | | | | |
| 15 | | | | | | | | | | | | | | | | | | | | | | | | | |
| 16 | | | | | | | | | | | | | | | | | | | | | | | | | |
| 17 | | | | | | | | | | | | | | | | | | | | | | | | | |
| 18 | | | | | | | | | | | | | | | | | | | | | | | | | |
| 19 | | | | | | | | | | | | | | | | | | | | | | | | | |
| 20 | | | | | | | | | | | | | | | | | | | | | | | | | |
| 21 | | | | | | | | | | | | | | | | | | | | | | | | | |
| 22 | | | | | | | | | | | | | | | | | | | | | | | | | |
| 23 | | | | | | | | | | | | | | | | | | | | | | | | | |
| 24 | | | | | | | | | | | | | | | | | | | | | | | | | |
| 25 | | | | | | | | | | | | | | | | | | | | | | | | | |
| 26 | | | | | | | | | | | | | | | | | | | | | | | | | |
| 27 | | | | | | | | | | | | | | | | | | | | | | | | | |
| 28 | | | | | | | | | | | | | | | | | | | | | | | | | |
| 29 | | | | | | | | | | | | | | | | | | | | | | | | | |
| 30 | | | | | | | | | | | | | | | | | | | | | | | | | |
| 31 | | | | | | | | | | | | | | | | | | | | | | | | | |
| 32 | | | | | | | | | | | | | | | | | | | | | | | | | |
| 33 | | | | | | | | | | | | | | | | | | | | | | | | | |
| 34 | | | | | | | | | | | | | | | | | | | | | | | | | |
| 35 | | | | | | | | | | | | | | | | | | | | | | | | | |
| 36 | | | | | | | | | | | | | | | | | | | | | | | | | |

# Period_____

| Week____ | | | | | Week____ | | | | | Week____ | | | | | Week____ | | | | | Week____ | | | | | | | Days Present | Days Absent | Tardies | Quarter Grade | | |
|---|---|---|---|---|---|---|---|---|---|---|---|---|---|---|---|---|---|---|---|---|---|---|---|---|---|---|---|---|---|---|---|
| M | T | W | T | F | M | T | W | T | F | M | T | W | T | F | M | T | W | T | F | M | T | W | T | F | | | | | | | |
| | | | | | | | | | | | | | | | | | | | | | | | | | | | | | | | |
| | | | | | | | | | | | | | | | | | | | | | | | | | | | | | | | |
| | | | | | | | | | | | | | | | | | | | | | | | | | 1 | | | | | | |
| | | | | | | | | | | | | | | | | | | | | | | | | | 2 | | | | | | |
| | | | | | | | | | | | | | | | | | | | | | | | | | 3 | | | | | | |
| | | | | | | | | | | | | | | | | | | | | | | | | | 4 | | | | | | |
| | | | | | | | | | | | | | | | | | | | | | | | | | 5 | | | | | | |
| | | | | | | | | | | | | | | | | | | | | | | | | | 6 | | | | | | |
| | | | | | | | | | | | | | | | | | | | | | | | | | 7 | | | | | | |
| | | | | | | | | | | | | | | | | | | | | | | | | | 8 | | | | | | |
| | | | | | | | | | | | | | | | | | | | | | | | | | 9 | | | | | | |
| | | | | | | | | | | | | | | | | | | | | | | | | | 10 | | | | | | |
| | | | | | | | | | | | | | | | | | | | | | | | | | 11 | | | | | | |
| | | | | | | | | | | | | | | | | | | | | | | | | | 12 | | | | | | |
| | | | | | | | | | | | | | | | | | | | | | | | | | 13 | | | | | | |
| | | | | | | | | | | | | | | | | | | | | | | | | | 14 | | | | | | |
| | | | | | | | | | | | | | | | | | | | | | | | | | 15 | | | | | | |
| | | | | | | | | | | | | | | | | | | | | | | | | | 16 | | | | | | |
| | | | | | | | | | | | | | | | | | | | | | | | | | 17 | | | | | | |
| | | | | | | | | | | | | | | | | | | | | | | | | | 18 | | | | | | |
| | | | | | | | | | | | | | | | | | | | | | | | | | 19 | | | | | | |
| | | | | | | | | | | | | | | | | | | | | | | | | | 20 | | | | | | |
| | | | | | | | | | | | | | | | | | | | | | | | | | 21 | | | | | | |
| | | | | | | | | | | | | | | | | | | | | | | | | | 22 | | | | | | |
| | | | | | | | | | | | | | | | | | | | | | | | | | 23 | | | | | | |
| | | | | | | | | | | | | | | | | | | | | | | | | | 24 | | | | | | |
| | | | | | | | | | | | | | | | | | | | | | | | | | 25 | | | | | | |
| | | | | | | | | | | | | | | | | | | | | | | | | | 26 | | | | | | |
| | | | | | | | | | | | | | | | | | | | | | | | | | 27 | | | | | | |
| | | | | | | | | | | | | | | | | | | | | | | | | | 28 | | | | | | |
| | | | | | | | | | | | | | | | | | | | | | | | | | 29 | | | | | | |
| | | | | | | | | | | | | | | | | | | | | | | | | | 30 | | | | | | |
| | | | | | | | | | | | | | | | | | | | | | | | | | 31 | | | | | | |
| | | | | | | | | | | | | | | | | | | | | | | | | | 32 | | | | | | |
| | | | | | | | | | | | | | | | | | | | | | | | | | 33 | | | | | | |
| | | | | | | | | | | | | | | | | | | | | | | | | | 34 | | | | | | |
| | | | | | | | | | | | | | | | | | | | | | | | | | 35 | | | | | | |
| | | | | | | | | | | | | | | | | | | | | | | | | | 36 | | | | | | |

# Subject_____

| Week | Week\_\_\_\_ | | | | | Week\_\_\_\_ | | | | | Week\_\_\_\_ | | | | | Week\_\_\_\_ | | | | | Week\_\_\_\_ | | | | |
|---|---|---|---|---|---|---|---|---|---|---|---|---|---|---|---|---|---|---|---|---|---|---|---|---|---|
| Day | M | T | W | T | F | M | T | W | T | F | M | T | W | T | F | M | T | W | T | F | M | T | W | T | F |
| Date | | | | | | | | | | | | | | | | | | | | | | | | | |
| Assignments or Attendance | | | | | | | | | | | | | | | | | | | | | | | | | |
| Name | | | | | | | | | | | | | | | | | | | | | | | | | |
| 1 | | | | | | | | | | | | | | | | | | | | | | | | | |
| 2 | | | | | | | | | | | | | | | | | | | | | | | | | |
| 3 | | | | | | | | | | | | | | | | | | | | | | | | | |
| 4 | | | | | | | | | | | | | | | | | | | | | | | | | |
| 5 | | | | | | | | | | | | | | | | | | | | | | | | | |
| 6 | | | | | | | | | | | | | | | | | | | | | | | | | |
| 7 | | | | | | | | | | | | | | | | | | | | | | | | | |
| 8 | | | | | | | | | | | | | | | | | | | | | | | | | |
| 9 | | | | | | | | | | | | | | | | | | | | | | | | | |
| 10 | | | | | | | | | | | | | | | | | | | | | | | | | |
| 11 | | | | | | | | | | | | | | | | | | | | | | | | | |
| 12 | | | | | | | | | | | | | | | | | | | | | | | | | |
| 13 | | | | | | | | | | | | | | | | | | | | | | | | | |
| 14 | | | | | | | | | | | | | | | | | | | | | | | | | |
| 15 | | | | | | | | | | | | | | | | | | | | | | | | | |
| 16 | | | | | | | | | | | | | | | | | | | | | | | | | |
| 17 | | | | | | | | | | | | | | | | | | | | | | | | | |
| 18 | | | | | | | | | | | | | | | | | | | | | | | | | |
| 19 | | | | | | | | | | | | | | | | | | | | | | | | | |
| 20 | | | | | | | | | | | | | | | | | | | | | | | | | |
| 21 | | | | | | | | | | | | | | | | | | | | | | | | | |
| 22 | | | | | | | | | | | | | | | | | | | | | | | | | |
| 23 | | | | | | | | | | | | | | | | | | | | | | | | | |
| 24 | | | | | | | | | | | | | | | | | | | | | | | | | |
| 25 | | | | | | | | | | | | | | | | | | | | | | | | | |
| 26 | | | | | | | | | | | | | | | | | | | | | | | | | |
| 27 | | | | | | | | | | | | | | | | | | | | | | | | | |
| 28 | | | | | | | | | | | | | | | | | | | | | | | | | |
| 29 | | | | | | | | | | | | | | | | | | | | | | | | | |
| 30 | | | | | | | | | | | | | | | | | | | | | | | | | |
| 31 | | | | | | | | | | | | | | | | | | | | | | | | | |
| 32 | | | | | | | | | | | | | | | | | | | | | | | | | |
| 33 | | | | | | | | | | | | | | | | | | | | | | | | | |
| 34 | | | | | | | | | | | | | | | | | | | | | | | | | |
| 35 | | | | | | | | | | | | | | | | | | | | | | | | | |
| 36 | | | | | | | | | | | | | | | | | | | | | | | | | |

# Period

| Week____ | | | | | Week____ | | | | | Week____ | | | | | Week____ | | | | | Week____ | | | | | | Days Present | Days Absent | Tardies | Quarter Grade | | |
|---|---|---|---|---|---|---|---|---|---|---|---|---|---|---|---|---|---|---|---|---|---|---|---|---|---|---|---|---|---|---|---|
| M | T | W | T | F | M | T | W | T | F | M | T | W | T | F | M | T | W | T | F | M | T | W | T | F | | | | | | | |
| | | | | | | | | | | | | | | | | | | | | | | | | | 1 | | | | | | |
| | | | | | | | | | | | | | | | | | | | | | | | | | 2 | | | | | | |
| | | | | | | | | | | | | | | | | | | | | | | | | | 3 | | | | | | |
| | | | | | | | | | | | | | | | | | | | | | | | | | 4 | | | | | | |
| | | | | | | | | | | | | | | | | | | | | | | | | | 5 | | | | | | |
| | | | | | | | | | | | | | | | | | | | | | | | | | 6 | | | | | | |
| | | | | | | | | | | | | | | | | | | | | | | | | | 7 | | | | | | |
| | | | | | | | | | | | | | | | | | | | | | | | | | 8 | | | | | | |
| | | | | | | | | | | | | | | | | | | | | | | | | | 9 | | | | | | |
| | | | | | | | | | | | | | | | | | | | | | | | | | 10 | | | | | | |
| | | | | | | | | | | | | | | | | | | | | | | | | | 11 | | | | | | |
| | | | | | | | | | | | | | | | | | | | | | | | | | 12 | | | | | | |
| | | | | | | | | | | | | | | | | | | | | | | | | | 13 | | | | | | |
| | | | | | | | | | | | | | | | | | | | | | | | | | 14 | | | | | | |
| | | | | | | | | | | | | | | | | | | | | | | | | | 15 | | | | | | |
| | | | | | | | | | | | | | | | | | | | | | | | | | 16 | | | | | | |
| | | | | | | | | | | | | | | | | | | | | | | | | | 17 | | | | | | |
| | | | | | | | | | | | | | | | | | | | | | | | | | 18 | | | | | | |
| | | | | | | | | | | | | | | | | | | | | | | | | | 19 | | | | | | |
| | | | | | | | | | | | | | | | | | | | | | | | | | 20 | | | | | | |
| | | | | | | | | | | | | | | | | | | | | | | | | | 21 | | | | | | |
| | | | | | | | | | | | | | | | | | | | | | | | | | 22 | | | | | | |
| | | | | | | | | | | | | | | | | | | | | | | | | | 23 | | | | | | |
| | | | | | | | | | | | | | | | | | | | | | | | | | 24 | | | | | | |
| | | | | | | | | | | | | | | | | | | | | | | | | | 25 | | | | | | |
| | | | | | | | | | | | | | | | | | | | | | | | | | 26 | | | | | | |
| | | | | | | | | | | | | | | | | | | | | | | | | | 27 | | | | | | |
| | | | | | | | | | | | | | | | | | | | | | | | | | 28 | | | | | | |
| | | | | | | | | | | | | | | | | | | | | | | | | | 29 | | | | | | |
| | | | | | | | | | | | | | | | | | | | | | | | | | 30 | | | | | | |
| | | | | | | | | | | | | | | | | | | | | | | | | | 31 | | | | | | |
| | | | | | | | | | | | | | | | | | | | | | | | | | 32 | | | | | | |
| | | | | | | | | | | | | | | | | | | | | | | | | | 33 | | | | | | |
| | | | | | | | | | | | | | | | | | | | | | | | | | 34 | | | | | | |
| | | | | | | | | | | | | | | | | | | | | | | | | | 35 | | | | | | |
| | | | | | | | | | | | | | | | | | | | | | | | | | 36 | | | | | | |

# Subject_____

| Week | Week____ | | | | | Week____ | | | | | Week____ | | | | | Week____ | | | | | Week____ | | | | |
|---|---|---|---|---|---|---|---|---|---|---|---|---|---|---|---|---|---|---|---|---|---|---|---|---|---|
| Day | M | T | W | T | F | M | T | W | T | F | M | T | W | T | F | M | T | W | T | F | M | T | W | T | F |
| Date | | | | | | | | | | | | | | | | | | | | | | | | | |
| Assignments or Attendance | | | | | | | | | | | | | | | | | | | | | | | | | |
| Name | | | | | | | | | | | | | | | | | | | | | | | | | |
| 1 | | | | | | | | | | | | | | | | | | | | | | | | | |
| 2 | | | | | | | | | | | | | | | | | | | | | | | | | |
| 3 | | | | | | | | | | | | | | | | | | | | | | | | | |
| 4 | | | | | | | | | | | | | | | | | | | | | | | | | |
| 5 | | | | | | | | | | | | | | | | | | | | | | | | | |
| 6 | | | | | | | | | | | | | | | | | | | | | | | | | |
| 7 | | | | | | | | | | | | | | | | | | | | | | | | | |
| 8 | | | | | | | | | | | | | | | | | | | | | | | | | |
| 9 | | | | | | | | | | | | | | | | | | | | | | | | | |
| 10 | | | | | | | | | | | | | | | | | | | | | | | | | |
| 11 | | | | | | | | | | | | | | | | | | | | | | | | | |
| 12 | | | | | | | | | | | | | | | | | | | | | | | | | |
| 13 | | | | | | | | | | | | | | | | | | | | | | | | | |
| 14 | | | | | | | | | | | | | | | | | | | | | | | | | |
| 15 | | | | | | | | | | | | | | | | | | | | | | | | | |
| 16 | | | | | | | | | | | | | | | | | | | | | | | | | |
| 17 | | | | | | | | | | | | | | | | | | | | | | | | | |
| 18 | | | | | | | | | | | | | | | | | | | | | | | | | |
| 19 | | | | | | | | | | | | | | | | | | | | | | | | | |
| 20 | | | | | | | | | | | | | | | | | | | | | | | | | |
| 21 | | | | | | | | | | | | | | | | | | | | | | | | | |
| 22 | | | | | | | | | | | | | | | | | | | | | | | | | |
| 23 | | | | | | | | | | | | | | | | | | | | | | | | | |
| 24 | | | | | | | | | | | | | | | | | | | | | | | | | |
| 25 | | | | | | | | | | | | | | | | | | | | | | | | | |
| 26 | | | | | | | | | | | | | | | | | | | | | | | | | |
| 27 | | | | | | | | | | | | | | | | | | | | | | | | | |
| 28 | | | | | | | | | | | | | | | | | | | | | | | | | |
| 29 | | | | | | | | | | | | | | | | | | | | | | | | | |
| 30 | | | | | | | | | | | | | | | | | | | | | | | | | |
| 31 | | | | | | | | | | | | | | | | | | | | | | | | | |
| 32 | | | | | | | | | | | | | | | | | | | | | | | | | |
| 33 | | | | | | | | | | | | | | | | | | | | | | | | | |
| 34 | | | | | | | | | | | | | | | | | | | | | | | | | |
| 35 | | | | | | | | | | | | | | | | | | | | | | | | | |
| 36 | | | | | | | | | | | | | | | | | | | | | | | | | |

# Period

| Week___ | | | | | Week___ | | | | | Week___ | | | | | Week___ | | | | | Week___ | | | | | | | Days Present | Days Absent | Tardies | Quarter Grade | | |
|---|---|---|---|---|---|---|---|---|---|---|---|---|---|---|---|---|---|---|---|---|---|---|---|---|---|---|---|---|---|---|---|---|
| M | T | W | T | F | M | T | W | T | F | M | T | W | T | F | M | T | W | T | F | M | T | W | T | F | | | | | | | | |
| | | | | | | | | | | | | | | | | | | | | | | | | | | | | | | | | |
| | | | | | | | | | | | | | | | | | | | | | | | | | 1 | | | | | | | |
| | | | | | | | | | | | | | | | | | | | | | | | | | 2 | | | | | | | |
| | | | | | | | | | | | | | | | | | | | | | | | | | 3 | | | | | | | |
| | | | | | | | | | | | | | | | | | | | | | | | | | 4 | | | | | | | |
| | | | | | | | | | | | | | | | | | | | | | | | | | 5 | | | | | | | |
| | | | | | | | | | | | | | | | | | | | | | | | | | 6 | | | | | | | |
| | | | | | | | | | | | | | | | | | | | | | | | | | 7 | | | | | | | |
| | | | | | | | | | | | | | | | | | | | | | | | | | 8 | | | | | | | |
| | | | | | | | | | | | | | | | | | | | | | | | | | 9 | | | | | | | |
| | | | | | | | | | | | | | | | | | | | | | | | | | 10 | | | | | | | |
| | | | | | | | | | | | | | | | | | | | | | | | | | 11 | | | | | | | |
| | | | | | | | | | | | | | | | | | | | | | | | | | 12 | | | | | | | |
| | | | | | | | | | | | | | | | | | | | | | | | | | 13 | | | | | | | |
| | | | | | | | | | | | | | | | | | | | | | | | | | 14 | | | | | | | |
| | | | | | | | | | | | | | | | | | | | | | | | | | 15 | | | | | | | |
| | | | | | | | | | | | | | | | | | | | | | | | | | 16 | | | | | | | |
| | | | | | | | | | | | | | | | | | | | | | | | | | 17 | | | | | | | |
| | | | | | | | | | | | | | | | | | | | | | | | | | 18 | | | | | | | |
| | | | | | | | | | | | | | | | | | | | | | | | | | 19 | | | | | | | |
| | | | | | | | | | | | | | | | | | | | | | | | | | 20 | | | | | | | |
| | | | | | | | | | | | | | | | | | | | | | | | | | 21 | | | | | | | |
| | | | | | | | | | | | | | | | | | | | | | | | | | 22 | | | | | | | |
| | | | | | | | | | | | | | | | | | | | | | | | | | 23 | | | | | | | |
| | | | | | | | | | | | | | | | | | | | | | | | | | 24 | | | | | | | |
| | | | | | | | | | | | | | | | | | | | | | | | | | 25 | | | | | | | |
| | | | | | | | | | | | | | | | | | | | | | | | | | 26 | | | | | | | |
| | | | | | | | | | | | | | | | | | | | | | | | | | 27 | | | | | | | |
| | | | | | | | | | | | | | | | | | | | | | | | | | 28 | | | | | | | |
| | | | | | | | | | | | | | | | | | | | | | | | | | 29 | | | | | | | |
| | | | | | | | | | | | | | | | | | | | | | | | | | 30 | | | | | | | |
| | | | | | | | | | | | | | | | | | | | | | | | | | 31 | | | | | | | |
| | | | | | | | | | | | | | | | | | | | | | | | | | 32 | | | | | | | |
| | | | | | | | | | | | | | | | | | | | | | | | | | 33 | | | | | | | |
| | | | | | | | | | | | | | | | | | | | | | | | | | 34 | | | | | | | |
| | | | | | | | | | | | | | | | | | | | | | | | | | 35 | | | | | | | |
| | | | | | | | | | | | | | | | | | | | | | | | | | 36 | | | | | | | |

# Subject_____

| Week | Week____ | | | | | Week____ | | | | | Week____ | | | | | Week____ | | | | | Week____ | | | | |
|---|---|---|---|---|---|---|---|---|---|---|---|---|---|---|---|---|---|---|---|---|---|---|---|---|---|
| Day | M | T | W | T | F | M | T | W | T | F | M | T | W | T | F | M | T | W | T | F | M | T | W | T | F |
| Date | | | | | | | | | | | | | | | | | | | | | | | | | |
| Assignments or Attendance | | | | | | | | | | | | | | | | | | | | | | | | | |
| Name | | | | | | | | | | | | | | | | | | | | | | | | | |
| 1 | | | | | | | | | | | | | | | | | | | | | | | | | |
| 2 | | | | | | | | | | | | | | | | | | | | | | | | | |
| 3 | | | | | | | | | | | | | | | | | | | | | | | | | |
| 4 | | | | | | | | | | | | | | | | | | | | | | | | | |
| 5 | | | | | | | | | | | | | | | | | | | | | | | | | |
| 6 | | | | | | | | | | | | | | | | | | | | | | | | | |
| 7 | | | | | | | | | | | | | | | | | | | | | | | | | |
| 8 | | | | | | | | | | | | | | | | | | | | | | | | | |
| 9 | | | | | | | | | | | | | | | | | | | | | | | | | |
| 10 | | | | | | | | | | | | | | | | | | | | | | | | | |
| 11 | | | | | | | | | | | | | | | | | | | | | | | | | |
| 12 | | | | | | | | | | | | | | | | | | | | | | | | | |
| 13 | | | | | | | | | | | | | | | | | | | | | | | | | |
| 14 | | | | | | | | | | | | | | | | | | | | | | | | | |
| 15 | | | | | | | | | | | | | | | | | | | | | | | | | |
| 16 | | | | | | | | | | | | | | | | | | | | | | | | | |
| 17 | | | | | | | | | | | | | | | | | | | | | | | | | |
| 18 | | | | | | | | | | | | | | | | | | | | | | | | | |
| 19 | | | | | | | | | | | | | | | | | | | | | | | | | |
| 20 | | | | | | | | | | | | | | | | | | | | | | | | | |
| 21 | | | | | | | | | | | | | | | | | | | | | | | | | |
| 22 | | | | | | | | | | | | | | | | | | | | | | | | | |
| 23 | | | | | | | | | | | | | | | | | | | | | | | | | |
| 24 | | | | | | | | | | | | | | | | | | | | | | | | | |
| 25 | | | | | | | | | | | | | | | | | | | | | | | | | |
| 26 | | | | | | | | | | | | | | | | | | | | | | | | | |
| 27 | | | | | | | | | | | | | | | | | | | | | | | | | |
| 28 | | | | | | | | | | | | | | | | | | | | | | | | | |
| 29 | | | | | | | | | | | | | | | | | | | | | | | | | |
| 30 | | | | | | | | | | | | | | | | | | | | | | | | | |
| 31 | | | | | | | | | | | | | | | | | | | | | | | | | |
| 32 | | | | | | | | | | | | | | | | | | | | | | | | | |
| 33 | | | | | | | | | | | | | | | | | | | | | | | | | |
| 34 | | | | | | | | | | | | | | | | | | | | | | | | | |
| 35 | | | | | | | | | | | | | | | | | | | | | | | | | |
| 36 | | | | | | | | | | | | | | | | | | | | | | | | | |

# Period

| M | T | W | T | F | M | T | W | T | F | M | T | W | T | F | M | T | W | T | F | M | T | W | T | F | | Days Present | Days Absent | Tardies | Quarter Grade | | |
|---|---|---|---|---|---|---|---|---|---|---|---|---|---|---|---|---|---|---|---|---|---|---|---|---|---|---|---|---|---|---|---|
| Week____ | | | | | Week____ | | | | | Week____ | | | | | Week____ | | | | | Week____ | | | | | | | | | | | |

| # | | | | | | | | | | | | | | | | | | | | | | | | | | Days Present | Days Absent | Tardies | Quarter Grade | | |
|---|---|---|---|---|---|---|---|---|---|---|---|---|---|---|---|---|---|---|---|---|---|---|---|---|---|---|---|---|---|---|---|
| 1 | | | | | | | | | | | | | | | | | | | | | | | | | | | | | | | |
| 2 | | | | | | | | | | | | | | | | | | | | | | | | | | | | | | | |
| 3 | | | | | | | | | | | | | | | | | | | | | | | | | | | | | | | |
| 4 | | | | | | | | | | | | | | | | | | | | | | | | | | | | | | | |
| 5 | | | | | | | | | | | | | | | | | | | | | | | | | | | | | | | |
| 6 | | | | | | | | | | | | | | | | | | | | | | | | | | | | | | | |
| 7 | | | | | | | | | | | | | | | | | | | | | | | | | | | | | | | |
| 8 | | | | | | | | | | | | | | | | | | | | | | | | | | | | | | | |
| 9 | | | | | | | | | | | | | | | | | | | | | | | | | | | | | | | |
| 10 | | | | | | | | | | | | | | | | | | | | | | | | | | | | | | | |
| 11 | | | | | | | | | | | | | | | | | | | | | | | | | | | | | | | |
| 12 | | | | | | | | | | | | | | | | | | | | | | | | | | | | | | | |
| 13 | | | | | | | | | | | | | | | | | | | | | | | | | | | | | | | |
| 14 | | | | | | | | | | | | | | | | | | | | | | | | | | | | | | | |
| 15 | | | | | | | | | | | | | | | | | | | | | | | | | | | | | | | |
| 16 | | | | | | | | | | | | | | | | | | | | | | | | | | | | | | | |
| 17 | | | | | | | | | | | | | | | | | | | | | | | | | | | | | | | |
| 18 | | | | | | | | | | | | | | | | | | | | | | | | | | | | | | | |
| 19 | | | | | | | | | | | | | | | | | | | | | | | | | | | | | | | |
| 20 | | | | | | | | | | | | | | | | | | | | | | | | | | | | | | | |
| 21 | | | | | | | | | | | | | | | | | | | | | | | | | | | | | | | |
| 22 | | | | | | | | | | | | | | | | | | | | | | | | | | | | | | | |
| 23 | | | | | | | | | | | | | | | | | | | | | | | | | | | | | | | |
| 24 | | | | | | | | | | | | | | | | | | | | | | | | | | | | | | | |
| 25 | | | | | | | | | | | | | | | | | | | | | | | | | | | | | | | |
| 26 | | | | | | | | | | | | | | | | | | | | | | | | | | | | | | | |
| 27 | | | | | | | | | | | | | | | | | | | | | | | | | | | | | | | |
| 28 | | | | | | | | | | | | | | | | | | | | | | | | | | | | | | | |
| 29 | | | | | | | | | | | | | | | | | | | | | | | | | | | | | | | |
| 30 | | | | | | | | | | | | | | | | | | | | | | | | | | | | | | | |
| 31 | | | | | | | | | | | | | | | | | | | | | | | | | | | | | | | |
| 32 | | | | | | | | | | | | | | | | | | | | | | | | | | | | | | | |
| 33 | | | | | | | | | | | | | | | | | | | | | | | | | | | | | | | |
| 34 | | | | | | | | | | | | | | | | | | | | | | | | | | | | | | | |
| 35 | | | | | | | | | | | | | | | | | | | | | | | | | | | | | | | |
| 36 | | | | | | | | | | | | | | | | | | | | | | | | | | | | | | | |

# Subject_____

| Week | Week____ | | | | | Week____ | | | | | Week____ | | | | | Week____ | | | | | Week____ | | | | |
|---|---|---|---|---|---|---|---|---|---|---|---|---|---|---|---|---|---|---|---|---|---|---|---|---|---|
| Day | M | T | W | T | F | M | T | W | T | F | M | T | W | T | F | M | T | W | T | F | M | T | W | T | F |
| Date | | | | | | | | | | | | | | | | | | | | | | | | | |
| Assignments or Attendance | | | | | | | | | | | | | | | | | | | | | | | | | |
| Name | | | | | | | | | | | | | | | | | | | | | | | | | |
| 1 | | | | | | | | | | | | | | | | | | | | | | | | | |
| 2 | | | | | | | | | | | | | | | | | | | | | | | | | |
| 3 | | | | | | | | | | | | | | | | | | | | | | | | | |
| 4 | | | | | | | | | | | | | | | | | | | | | | | | | |
| 5 | | | | | | | | | | | | | | | | | | | | | | | | | |
| 6 | | | | | | | | | | | | | | | | | | | | | | | | | |
| 7 | | | | | | | | | | | | | | | | | | | | | | | | | |
| 8 | | | | | | | | | | | | | | | | | | | | | | | | | |
| 9 | | | | | | | | | | | | | | | | | | | | | | | | | |
| 10 | | | | | | | | | | | | | | | | | | | | | | | | | |
| 11 | | | | | | | | | | | | | | | | | | | | | | | | | |
| 12 | | | | | | | | | | | | | | | | | | | | | | | | | |
| 13 | | | | | | | | | | | | | | | | | | | | | | | | | |
| 14 | | | | | | | | | | | | | | | | | | | | | | | | | |
| 15 | | | | | | | | | | | | | | | | | | | | | | | | | |
| 16 | | | | | | | | | | | | | | | | | | | | | | | | | |
| 17 | | | | | | | | | | | | | | | | | | | | | | | | | |
| 18 | | | | | | | | | | | | | | | | | | | | | | | | | |
| 19 | | | | | | | | | | | | | | | | | | | | | | | | | |
| 20 | | | | | | | | | | | | | | | | | | | | | | | | | |
| 21 | | | | | | | | | | | | | | | | | | | | | | | | | |
| 22 | | | | | | | | | | | | | | | | | | | | | | | | | |
| 23 | | | | | | | | | | | | | | | | | | | | | | | | | |
| 24 | | | | | | | | | | | | | | | | | | | | | | | | | |
| 25 | | | | | | | | | | | | | | | | | | | | | | | | | |
| 26 | | | | | | | | | | | | | | | | | | | | | | | | | |
| 27 | | | | | | | | | | | | | | | | | | | | | | | | | |
| 28 | | | | | | | | | | | | | | | | | | | | | | | | | |
| 29 | | | | | | | | | | | | | | | | | | | | | | | | | |
| 30 | | | | | | | | | | | | | | | | | | | | | | | | | |
| 31 | | | | | | | | | | | | | | | | | | | | | | | | | |
| 32 | | | | | | | | | | | | | | | | | | | | | | | | | |
| 33 | | | | | | | | | | | | | | | | | | | | | | | | | |
| 34 | | | | | | | | | | | | | | | | | | | | | | | | | |
| 35 | | | | | | | | | | | | | | | | | | | | | | | | | |
| 36 | | | | | | | | | | | | | | | | | | | | | | | | | |

# Period_____

| Week____ | | | | | Week____ | | | | | Week____ | | | | | Week____ | | | | | Week____ | | | | | | Days Present | Days Absent | Tardies | Quarter Grade | |
|---|---|---|---|---|---|---|---|---|---|---|---|---|---|---|---|---|---|---|---|---|---|---|---|---|---|---|---|---|---|---|
| M | T | W | T | F | M | T | W | T | F | M | T | W | T | F | M | T | W | T | F | M | T | W | T | F | | | | | | |
| | | | | | | | | | | | | | | | | | | | | | | | | | | | | | | |
| | | | | | | | | | | | | | | | | | | | | | | | | | | | | | | |
| | | | | | | | | | | | | | | | | | | | | | | | | | | | | | | |
| | | | | | | | | | | | | | | | | | | | | | | | | | 1 | | | | | |
| | | | | | | | | | | | | | | | | | | | | | | | | | 2 | | | | | |
| | | | | | | | | | | | | | | | | | | | | | | | | | 3 | | | | | |
| | | | | | | | | | | | | | | | | | | | | | | | | | 4 | | | | | |
| | | | | | | | | | | | | | | | | | | | | | | | | | 5 | | | | | |
| | | | | | | | | | | | | | | | | | | | | | | | | | 6 | | | | | |
| | | | | | | | | | | | | | | | | | | | | | | | | | 7 | | | | | |
| | | | | | | | | | | | | | | | | | | | | | | | | | 8 | | | | | |
| | | | | | | | | | | | | | | | | | | | | | | | | | 9 | | | | | |
| | | | | | | | | | | | | | | | | | | | | | | | | | 10 | | | | | |
| | | | | | | | | | | | | | | | | | | | | | | | | | 11 | | | | | |
| | | | | | | | | | | | | | | | | | | | | | | | | | 12 | | | | | |
| | | | | | | | | | | | | | | | | | | | | | | | | | 13 | | | | | |
| | | | | | | | | | | | | | | | | | | | | | | | | | 14 | | | | | |
| | | | | | | | | | | | | | | | | | | | | | | | | | 15 | | | | | |
| | | | | | | | | | | | | | | | | | | | | | | | | | 16 | | | | | |
| | | | | | | | | | | | | | | | | | | | | | | | | | 17 | | | | | |
| | | | | | | | | | | | | | | | | | | | | | | | | | 18 | | | | | |
| | | | | | | | | | | | | | | | | | | | | | | | | | 19 | | | | | |
| | | | | | | | | | | | | | | | | | | | | | | | | | 20 | | | | | |
| | | | | | | | | | | | | | | | | | | | | | | | | | 21 | | | | | |
| | | | | | | | | | | | | | | | | | | | | | | | | | 22 | | | | | |
| | | | | | | | | | | | | | | | | | | | | | | | | | 23 | | | | | |
| | | | | | | | | | | | | | | | | | | | | | | | | | 24 | | | | | |
| | | | | | | | | | | | | | | | | | | | | | | | | | 25 | | | | | |
| | | | | | | | | | | | | | | | | | | | | | | | | | 26 | | | | | |
| | | | | | | | | | | | | | | | | | | | | | | | | | 27 | | | | | |
| | | | | | | | | | | | | | | | | | | | | | | | | | 28 | | | | | |
| | | | | | | | | | | | | | | | | | | | | | | | | | 29 | | | | | |
| | | | | | | | | | | | | | | | | | | | | | | | | | 30 | | | | | |
| | | | | | | | | | | | | | | | | | | | | | | | | | 31 | | | | | |
| | | | | | | | | | | | | | | | | | | | | | | | | | 32 | | | | | |
| | | | | | | | | | | | | | | | | | | | | | | | | | 33 | | | | | |
| | | | | | | | | | | | | | | | | | | | | | | | | | 34 | | | | | |
| | | | | | | | | | | | | | | | | | | | | | | | | | 35 | | | | | |
| | | | | | | | | | | | | | | | | | | | | | | | | | 36 | | | | | |

# Subject_____

| Week | Week____ | | | | | Week____ | | | | | Week____ | | | | | Week____ | | | | | Week____ | | | | |
|---|---|---|---|---|---|---|---|---|---|---|---|---|---|---|---|---|---|---|---|---|---|---|---|---|---|
| Day | M | T | W | T | F | M | T | W | T | F | M | T | W | T | F | M | T | W | T | F | M | T | W | T | F |
| Date | | | | | | | | | | | | | | | | | | | | | | | | | |
| Assignments or Attendance | | | | | | | | | | | | | | | | | | | | | | | | | |
| Name | | | | | | | | | | | | | | | | | | | | | | | | | |
| 1 | | | | | | | | | | | | | | | | | | | | | | | | | |
| 2 | | | | | | | | | | | | | | | | | | | | | | | | | |
| 3 | | | | | | | | | | | | | | | | | | | | | | | | | |
| 4 | | | | | | | | | | | | | | | | | | | | | | | | | |
| 5 | | | | | | | | | | | | | | | | | | | | | | | | | |
| 6 | | | | | | | | | | | | | | | | | | | | | | | | | |
| 7 | | | | | | | | | | | | | | | | | | | | | | | | | |
| 8 | | | | | | | | | | | | | | | | | | | | | | | | | |
| 9 | | | | | | | | | | | | | | | | | | | | | | | | | |
| 10 | | | | | | | | | | | | | | | | | | | | | | | | | |
| 11 | | | | | | | | | | | | | | | | | | | | | | | | | |
| 12 | | | | | | | | | | | | | | | | | | | | | | | | | |
| 13 | | | | | | | | | | | | | | | | | | | | | | | | | |
| 14 | | | | | | | | | | | | | | | | | | | | | | | | | |
| 15 | | | | | | | | | | | | | | | | | | | | | | | | | |
| 16 | | | | | | | | | | | | | | | | | | | | | | | | | |
| 17 | | | | | | | | | | | | | | | | | | | | | | | | | |
| 18 | | | | | | | | | | | | | | | | | | | | | | | | | |
| 19 | | | | | | | | | | | | | | | | | | | | | | | | | |
| 20 | | | | | | | | | | | | | | | | | | | | | | | | | |
| 21 | | | | | | | | | | | | | | | | | | | | | | | | | |
| 22 | | | | | | | | | | | | | | | | | | | | | | | | | |
| 23 | | | | | | | | | | | | | | | | | | | | | | | | | |
| 24 | | | | | | | | | | | | | | | | | | | | | | | | | |
| 25 | | | | | | | | | | | | | | | | | | | | | | | | | |
| 26 | | | | | | | | | | | | | | | | | | | | | | | | | |
| 27 | | | | | | | | | | | | | | | | | | | | | | | | | |
| 28 | | | | | | | | | | | | | | | | | | | | | | | | | |
| 29 | | | | | | | | | | | | | | | | | | | | | | | | | |
| 30 | | | | | | | | | | | | | | | | | | | | | | | | | |
| 31 | | | | | | | | | | | | | | | | | | | | | | | | | |
| 32 | | | | | | | | | | | | | | | | | | | | | | | | | |
| 33 | | | | | | | | | | | | | | | | | | | | | | | | | |
| 34 | | | | | | | | | | | | | | | | | | | | | | | | | |
| 35 | | | | | | | | | | | | | | | | | | | | | | | | | |
| 36 | | | | | | | | | | | | | | | | | | | | | | | | | |

# Period

| Week____ | | | | | Week____ | | | | | Week____ | | | | | Week____ | | | | | Week____ | | | | | | Days Present | Days Absent | Tardies | Quarter Grade | |
|---|---|---|---|---|---|---|---|---|---|---|---|---|---|---|---|---|---|---|---|---|---|---|---|---|---|---|---|---|---|---|
| M | T | W | T | F | M | T | W | T | F | M | T | W | T | F | M | T | W | T | F | M | T | W | T | F | | | | | | |
| | | | | | | | | | | | | | | | | | | | | | | | | | 1 | | | | | |
| | | | | | | | | | | | | | | | | | | | | | | | | | 2 | | | | | |
| | | | | | | | | | | | | | | | | | | | | | | | | | 3 | | | | | |
| | | | | | | | | | | | | | | | | | | | | | | | | | 4 | | | | | |
| | | | | | | | | | | | | | | | | | | | | | | | | | 5 | | | | | |
| | | | | | | | | | | | | | | | | | | | | | | | | | 6 | | | | | |
| | | | | | | | | | | | | | | | | | | | | | | | | | 7 | | | | | |
| | | | | | | | | | | | | | | | | | | | | | | | | | 8 | | | | | |
| | | | | | | | | | | | | | | | | | | | | | | | | | 9 | | | | | |
| | | | | | | | | | | | | | | | | | | | | | | | | | 10 | | | | | |
| | | | | | | | | | | | | | | | | | | | | | | | | | 11 | | | | | |
| | | | | | | | | | | | | | | | | | | | | | | | | | 12 | | | | | |
| | | | | | | | | | | | | | | | | | | | | | | | | | 13 | | | | | |
| | | | | | | | | | | | | | | | | | | | | | | | | | 14 | | | | | |
| | | | | | | | | | | | | | | | | | | | | | | | | | 15 | | | | | |
| | | | | | | | | | | | | | | | | | | | | | | | | | 16 | | | | | |
| | | | | | | | | | | | | | | | | | | | | | | | | | 17 | | | | | |
| | | | | | | | | | | | | | | | | | | | | | | | | | 18 | | | | | |
| | | | | | | | | | | | | | | | | | | | | | | | | | 19 | | | | | |
| | | | | | | | | | | | | | | | | | | | | | | | | | 20 | | | | | |
| | | | | | | | | | | | | | | | | | | | | | | | | | 21 | | | | | |
| | | | | | | | | | | | | | | | | | | | | | | | | | 22 | | | | | |
| | | | | | | | | | | | | | | | | | | | | | | | | | 23 | | | | | |
| | | | | | | | | | | | | | | | | | | | | | | | | | 24 | | | | | |
| | | | | | | | | | | | | | | | | | | | | | | | | | 25 | | | | | |
| | | | | | | | | | | | | | | | | | | | | | | | | | 26 | | | | | |
| | | | | | | | | | | | | | | | | | | | | | | | | | 27 | | | | | |
| | | | | | | | | | | | | | | | | | | | | | | | | | 28 | | | | | |
| | | | | | | | | | | | | | | | | | | | | | | | | | 29 | | | | | |
| | | | | | | | | | | | | | | | | | | | | | | | | | 30 | | | | | |
| | | | | | | | | | | | | | | | | | | | | | | | | | 31 | | | | | |
| | | | | | | | | | | | | | | | | | | | | | | | | | 32 | | | | | |
| | | | | | | | | | | | | | | | | | | | | | | | | | 33 | | | | | |
| | | | | | | | | | | | | | | | | | | | | | | | | | 34 | | | | | |
| | | | | | | | | | | | | | | | | | | | | | | | | | 35 | | | | | |
| | | | | | | | | | | | | | | | | | | | | | | | | | 36 | | | | | |

# Subject_____

| Week | Week____ | | | | Week____ | | | | Week____ | | | | Week____ | | | | Week____ | | | |
|---|---|---|---|---|---|---|---|---|---|---|---|---|---|---|---|---|---|---|---|---|
| Day | M | T | W | T | F | M | T | W | T | F | M | T | W | T | F | M | T | W | T | F | M | T | W | T | F |
| Date | | | | | | | | | | | | | | | | | | | | | | | | | |
| Assignments or Attendance | | | | | | | | | | | | | | | | | | | | | | | | | |
| Name | | | | | | | | | | | | | | | | | | | | | | | | | |
| 1 | | | | | | | | | | | | | | | | | | | | | | | | | |
| 2 | | | | | | | | | | | | | | | | | | | | | | | | | |
| 3 | | | | | | | | | | | | | | | | | | | | | | | | | |
| 4 | | | | | | | | | | | | | | | | | | | | | | | | | |
| 5 | | | | | | | | | | | | | | | | | | | | | | | | | |
| 6 | | | | | | | | | | | | | | | | | | | | | | | | | |
| 7 | | | | | | | | | | | | | | | | | | | | | | | | | |
| 8 | | | | | | | | | | | | | | | | | | | | | | | | | |
| 9 | | | | | | | | | | | | | | | | | | | | | | | | | |
| 10 | | | | | | | | | | | | | | | | | | | | | | | | | |
| 11 | | | | | | | | | | | | | | | | | | | | | | | | | |
| 12 | | | | | | | | | | | | | | | | | | | | | | | | | |
| 13 | | | | | | | | | | | | | | | | | | | | | | | | | |
| 14 | | | | | | | | | | | | | | | | | | | | | | | | | |
| 15 | | | | | | | | | | | | | | | | | | | | | | | | | |
| 16 | | | | | | | | | | | | | | | | | | | | | | | | | |
| 17 | | | | | | | | | | | | | | | | | | | | | | | | | |
| 18 | | | | | | | | | | | | | | | | | | | | | | | | | |
| 19 | | | | | | | | | | | | | | | | | | | | | | | | | |
| 20 | | | | | | | | | | | | | | | | | | | | | | | | | |
| 21 | | | | | | | | | | | | | | | | | | | | | | | | | |
| 22 | | | | | | | | | | | | | | | | | | | | | | | | | |
| 23 | | | | | | | | | | | | | | | | | | | | | | | | | |
| 24 | | | | | | | | | | | | | | | | | | | | | | | | | |
| 25 | | | | | | | | | | | | | | | | | | | | | | | | | |
| 26 | | | | | | | | | | | | | | | | | | | | | | | | | |
| 27 | | | | | | | | | | | | | | | | | | | | | | | | | |
| 28 | | | | | | | | | | | | | | | | | | | | | | | | | |
| 29 | | | | | | | | | | | | | | | | | | | | | | | | | |
| 30 | | | | | | | | | | | | | | | | | | | | | | | | | |
| 31 | | | | | | | | | | | | | | | | | | | | | | | | | |
| 32 | | | | | | | | | | | | | | | | | | | | | | | | | |
| 33 | | | | | | | | | | | | | | | | | | | | | | | | | |
| 34 | | | | | | | | | | | | | | | | | | | | | | | | | |
| 35 | | | | | | | | | | | | | | | | | | | | | | | | | |
| 36 | | | | | | | | | | | | | | | | | | | | | | | | | |

# Period_____

| Week____ | | | | | Week____ | | | | | Week____ | | | | | Week____ | | | | | Week____ | | | | | | Days Present | Days Absent | Tardies | Quarter Grade | |
|---|---|---|---|---|---|---|---|---|---|---|---|---|---|---|---|---|---|---|---|---|---|---|---|---|---|---|---|---|---|---|---|
| M | T | W | T | F | M | T | W | T | F | M | T | W | T | F | M | T | W | T | F | M | T | W | T | F | | | | | | |
| | | | | | | | | | | | | | | | | | | | | | | | | | 1 | | | | | |
| | | | | | | | | | | | | | | | | | | | | | | | | | 2 | | | | | |
| | | | | | | | | | | | | | | | | | | | | | | | | | 3 | | | | | |
| | | | | | | | | | | | | | | | | | | | | | | | | | 4 | | | | | |
| | | | | | | | | | | | | | | | | | | | | | | | | | 5 | | | | | |
| | | | | | | | | | | | | | | | | | | | | | | | | | 6 | | | | | |
| | | | | | | | | | | | | | | | | | | | | | | | | | 7 | | | | | |
| | | | | | | | | | | | | | | | | | | | | | | | | | 8 | | | | | |
| | | | | | | | | | | | | | | | | | | | | | | | | | 9 | | | | | |
| | | | | | | | | | | | | | | | | | | | | | | | | | 10 | | | | | |
| | | | | | | | | | | | | | | | | | | | | | | | | | 11 | | | | | |
| | | | | | | | | | | | | | | | | | | | | | | | | | 12 | | | | | |
| | | | | | | | | | | | | | | | | | | | | | | | | | 13 | | | | | |
| | | | | | | | | | | | | | | | | | | | | | | | | | 14 | | | | | |
| | | | | | | | | | | | | | | | | | | | | | | | | | 15 | | | | | |
| | | | | | | | | | | | | | | | | | | | | | | | | | 16 | | | | | |
| | | | | | | | | | | | | | | | | | | | | | | | | | 17 | | | | | |
| | | | | | | | | | | | | | | | | | | | | | | | | | 18 | | | | | |
| | | | | | | | | | | | | | | | | | | | | | | | | | 19 | | | | | |
| | | | | | | | | | | | | | | | | | | | | | | | | | 20 | | | | | |
| | | | | | | | | | | | | | | | | | | | | | | | | | 21 | | | | | |
| | | | | | | | | | | | | | | | | | | | | | | | | | 22 | | | | | |
| | | | | | | | | | | | | | | | | | | | | | | | | | 23 | | | | | |
| | | | | | | | | | | | | | | | | | | | | | | | | | 24 | | | | | |
| | | | | | | | | | | | | | | | | | | | | | | | | | 25 | | | | | |
| | | | | | | | | | | | | | | | | | | | | | | | | | 26 | | | | | |
| | | | | | | | | | | | | | | | | | | | | | | | | | 27 | | | | | |
| | | | | | | | | | | | | | | | | | | | | | | | | | 28 | | | | | |
| | | | | | | | | | | | | | | | | | | | | | | | | | 29 | | | | | |
| | | | | | | | | | | | | | | | | | | | | | | | | | 30 | | | | | |
| | | | | | | | | | | | | | | | | | | | | | | | | | 31 | | | | | |
| | | | | | | | | | | | | | | | | | | | | | | | | | 32 | | | | | |
| | | | | | | | | | | | | | | | | | | | | | | | | | 33 | | | | | |
| | | | | | | | | | | | | | | | | | | | | | | | | | 34 | | | | | |
| | | | | | | | | | | | | | | | | | | | | | | | | | 35 | | | | | |
| | | | | | | | | | | | | | | | | | | | | | | | | | 36 | | | | | |

# Subject_____

| Week _____ | Week____ | | | | Week____ | | | | Week____ | | | | Week____ | | | | Week____ | | | |
|---|---|---|---|---|---|---|---|---|---|---|---|---|---|---|---|---|---|---|---|---|
| Day _____ | M | T | W | T | F | M | T | W | T | F | M | T | W | T | F | M | T | W | T | F | M | T | W | T | F |
| Date | | | | | | | | | | | | | | | | | | | | | | | | | |
| Assignments or Attendance | | | | | | | | | | | | | | | | | | | | | | | | | |
| Name | | | | | | | | | | | | | | | | | | | | | | | | | |
| 1 | | | | | | | | | | | | | | | | | | | | | | | | | |
| 2 | | | | | | | | | | | | | | | | | | | | | | | | | |
| 3 | | | | | | | | | | | | | | | | | | | | | | | | | |
| 4 | | | | | | | | | | | | | | | | | | | | | | | | | |
| 5 | | | | | | | | | | | | | | | | | | | | | | | | | |
| 6 | | | | | | | | | | | | | | | | | | | | | | | | | |
| 7 | | | | | | | | | | | | | | | | | | | | | | | | | |
| 8 | | | | | | | | | | | | | | | | | | | | | | | | | |
| 9 | | | | | | | | | | | | | | | | | | | | | | | | | |
| 10 | | | | | | | | | | | | | | | | | | | | | | | | | |
| 11 | | | | | | | | | | | | | | | | | | | | | | | | | |
| 12 | | | | | | | | | | | | | | | | | | | | | | | | | |
| 13 | | | | | | | | | | | | | | | | | | | | | | | | | |
| 14 | | | | | | | | | | | | | | | | | | | | | | | | | |
| 15 | | | | | | | | | | | | | | | | | | | | | | | | | |
| 16 | | | | | | | | | | | | | | | | | | | | | | | | | |
| 17 | | | | | | | | | | | | | | | | | | | | | | | | | |
| 18 | | | | | | | | | | | | | | | | | | | | | | | | | |
| 19 | | | | | | | | | | | | | | | | | | | | | | | | | |
| 20 | | | | | | | | | | | | | | | | | | | | | | | | | |
| 21 | | | | | | | | | | | | | | | | | | | | | | | | | |
| 22 | | | | | | | | | | | | | | | | | | | | | | | | | |
| 23 | | | | | | | | | | | | | | | | | | | | | | | | | |
| 24 | | | | | | | | | | | | | | | | | | | | | | | | | |
| 25 | | | | | | | | | | | | | | | | | | | | | | | | | |
| 26 | | | | | | | | | | | | | | | | | | | | | | | | | |
| 27 | | | | | | | | | | | | | | | | | | | | | | | | | |
| 28 | | | | | | | | | | | | | | | | | | | | | | | | | |
| 29 | | | | | | | | | | | | | | | | | | | | | | | | | |
| 30 | | | | | | | | | | | | | | | | | | | | | | | | | |
| 31 | | | | | | | | | | | | | | | | | | | | | | | | | |
| 32 | | | | | | | | | | | | | | | | | | | | | | | | | |
| 33 | | | | | | | | | | | | | | | | | | | | | | | | | |
| 34 | | | | | | | | | | | | | | | | | | | | | | | | | |
| 35 | | | | | | | | | | | | | | | | | | | | | | | | | |
| 36 | | | | | | | | | | | | | | | | | | | | | | | | | |

# Period _____

| Week ____ | | | | | Week ____ | | | | | Week ____ | | | | | Week ____ | | | | | Week ____ | | | | | | Days Present | Days Absent | Tardies | Quarter Grade | |
|---|---|---|---|---|---|---|---|---|---|---|---|---|---|---|---|---|---|---|---|---|---|---|---|---|---|---|---|---|---|
| M | T | W | T | F | M | T | W | T | F | M | T | W | T | F | M | T | W | T | F | M | T | W | T | F | | | | | | |
| | | | | | | | | | | | | | | | | | | | | | | | | | | | | | | |
| | | | | | | | | | | | | | | | | | | | | | | | | | 1 | | | | | |
| | | | | | | | | | | | | | | | | | | | | | | | | | 2 | | | | | |
| | | | | | | | | | | | | | | | | | | | | | | | | | 3 | | | | | |
| | | | | | | | | | | | | | | | | | | | | | | | | | 4 | | | | | |
| | | | | | | | | | | | | | | | | | | | | | | | | | 5 | | | | | |
| | | | | | | | | | | | | | | | | | | | | | | | | | 6 | | | | | |
| | | | | | | | | | | | | | | | | | | | | | | | | | 7 | | | | | |
| | | | | | | | | | | | | | | | | | | | | | | | | | 8 | | | | | |
| | | | | | | | | | | | | | | | | | | | | | | | | | 9 | | | | | |
| | | | | | | | | | | | | | | | | | | | | | | | | | 10 | | | | | |
| | | | | | | | | | | | | | | | | | | | | | | | | | 11 | | | | | |
| | | | | | | | | | | | | | | | | | | | | | | | | | 12 | | | | | |
| | | | | | | | | | | | | | | | | | | | | | | | | | 13 | | | | | |
| | | | | | | | | | | | | | | | | | | | | | | | | | 14 | | | | | |
| | | | | | | | | | | | | | | | | | | | | | | | | | 15 | | | | | |
| | | | | | | | | | | | | | | | | | | | | | | | | | 16 | | | | | |
| | | | | | | | | | | | | | | | | | | | | | | | | | 17 | | | | | |
| | | | | | | | | | | | | | | | | | | | | | | | | | 18 | | | | | |
| | | | | | | | | | | | | | | | | | | | | | | | | | 19 | | | | | |
| | | | | | | | | | | | | | | | | | | | | | | | | | 20 | | | | | |
| | | | | | | | | | | | | | | | | | | | | | | | | | 21 | | | | | |
| | | | | | | | | | | | | | | | | | | | | | | | | | 22 | | | | | |
| | | | | | | | | | | | | | | | | | | | | | | | | | 23 | | | | | |
| | | | | | | | | | | | | | | | | | | | | | | | | | 24 | | | | | |
| | | | | | | | | | | | | | | | | | | | | | | | | | 25 | | | | | |
| | | | | | | | | | | | | | | | | | | | | | | | | | 26 | | | | | |
| | | | | | | | | | | | | | | | | | | | | | | | | | 27 | | | | | |
| | | | | | | | | | | | | | | | | | | | | | | | | | 28 | | | | | |
| | | | | | | | | | | | | | | | | | | | | | | | | | 29 | | | | | |
| | | | | | | | | | | | | | | | | | | | | | | | | | 30 | | | | | |
| | | | | | | | | | | | | | | | | | | | | | | | | | 31 | | | | | |
| | | | | | | | | | | | | | | | | | | | | | | | | | 32 | | | | | |
| | | | | | | | | | | | | | | | | | | | | | | | | | 33 | | | | | |
| | | | | | | | | | | | | | | | | | | | | | | | | | 34 | | | | | |
| | | | | | | | | | | | | | | | | | | | | | | | | | 35 | | | | | |
| | | | | | | | | | | | | | | | | | | | | | | | | | 36 | | | | | |

# Subject_____

| Week | Week____ | | | | | Week____ | | | | | Week____ | | | | | Week____ | | | | | Week____ | | | | | Week____ | | | | |
|---|---|---|---|---|---|---|---|---|---|---|---|---|---|---|---|---|---|---|---|---|---|---|---|---|---|---|---|---|---|---|
| Day | M | T | W | T | F | M | T | W | T | F | M | T | W | T | F | M | T | W | T | F | M | T | W | T | F | M | T | W | T | F |
| Date | | | | | | | | | | | | | | | | | | | | | | | | | | | | | | |
| Assignments or Attendance | | | | | | | | | | | | | | | | | | | | | | | | | | | | | | |
| Name | | | | | | | | | | | | | | | | | | | | | | | | | | | | | | |
| 1 | | | | | | | | | | | | | | | | | | | | | | | | | | | | | | |
| 2 | | | | | | | | | | | | | | | | | | | | | | | | | | | | | | |
| 3 | | | | | | | | | | | | | | | | | | | | | | | | | | | | | | |
| 4 | | | | | | | | | | | | | | | | | | | | | | | | | | | | | | |
| 5 | | | | | | | | | | | | | | | | | | | | | | | | | | | | | | |
| 6 | | | | | | | | | | | | | | | | | | | | | | | | | | | | | | |
| 7 | | | | | | | | | | | | | | | | | | | | | | | | | | | | | | |
| 8 | | | | | | | | | | | | | | | | | | | | | | | | | | | | | | |
| 9 | | | | | | | | | | | | | | | | | | | | | | | | | | | | | | |
| 10 | | | | | | | | | | | | | | | | | | | | | | | | | | | | | | |
| 11 | | | | | | | | | | | | | | | | | | | | | | | | | | | | | | |
| 12 | | | | | | | | | | | | | | | | | | | | | | | | | | | | | | |
| 13 | | | | | | | | | | | | | | | | | | | | | | | | | | | | | | |
| 14 | | | | | | | | | | | | | | | | | | | | | | | | | | | | | | |
| 15 | | | | | | | | | | | | | | | | | | | | | | | | | | | | | | |
| 16 | | | | | | | | | | | | | | | | | | | | | | | | | | | | | | |
| 17 | | | | | | | | | | | | | | | | | | | | | | | | | | | | | | |
| 18 | | | | | | | | | | | | | | | | | | | | | | | | | | | | | | |
| 19 | | | | | | | | | | | | | | | | | | | | | | | | | | | | | | |
| 20 | | | | | | | | | | | | | | | | | | | | | | | | | | | | | | |
| 21 | | | | | | | | | | | | | | | | | | | | | | | | | | | | | | |
| 22 | | | | | | | | | | | | | | | | | | | | | | | | | | | | | | |
| 23 | | | | | | | | | | | | | | | | | | | | | | | | | | | | | | |
| 24 | | | | | | | | | | | | | | | | | | | | | | | | | | | | | | |
| 25 | | | | | | | | | | | | | | | | | | | | | | | | | | | | | | |
| 26 | | | | | | | | | | | | | | | | | | | | | | | | | | | | | | |
| 27 | | | | | | | | | | | | | | | | | | | | | | | | | | | | | | |
| 28 | | | | | | | | | | | | | | | | | | | | | | | | | | | | | | |
| 29 | | | | | | | | | | | | | | | | | | | | | | | | | | | | | | |
| 30 | | | | | | | | | | | | | | | | | | | | | | | | | | | | | | |
| 31 | | | | | | | | | | | | | | | | | | | | | | | | | | | | | | |
| 32 | | | | | | | | | | | | | | | | | | | | | | | | | | | | | | |
| 33 | | | | | | | | | | | | | | | | | | | | | | | | | | | | | | |
| 34 | | | | | | | | | | | | | | | | | | | | | | | | | | | | | | |
| 35 | | | | | | | | | | | | | | | | | | | | | | | | | | | | | | |
| 36 | | | | | | | | | | | | | | | | | | | | | | | | | | | | | | |

# Period

| | Week____ | | | | Week____ | | | | Week____ | | | | Week____ | | | | Week____ | | | | | Days Present | Days Absent | Tardies | Quarter Grade | |
|M|T|W|T|F|M|T|W|T|F|M|T|W|T|F|M|T|W|T|F|M|T|W|T|F| | | | | | |
|---|---|---|---|---|---|---|---|---|---|---|---|---|---|---|---|---|---|---|---|---|---|---|---|---|---|---|---|---|---|---|
| | | | | | | | | | | | | | | | | | | | | | | | | | 1 | | | | | |
| | | | | | | | | | | | | | | | | | | | | | | | | | 2 | | | | | |
| | | | | | | | | | | | | | | | | | | | | | | | | | 3 | | | | | |
| | | | | | | | | | | | | | | | | | | | | | | | | | 4 | | | | | |
| | | | | | | | | | | | | | | | | | | | | | | | | | 5 | | | | | |
| | | | | | | | | | | | | | | | | | | | | | | | | | 6 | | | | | |
| | | | | | | | | | | | | | | | | | | | | | | | | | 7 | | | | | |
| | | | | | | | | | | | | | | | | | | | | | | | | | 8 | | | | | |
| | | | | | | | | | | | | | | | | | | | | | | | | | 9 | | | | | |
| | | | | | | | | | | | | | | | | | | | | | | | | | 10 | | | | | |
| | | | | | | | | | | | | | | | | | | | | | | | | | 11 | | | | | |
| | | | | | | | | | | | | | | | | | | | | | | | | | 12 | | | | | |
| | | | | | | | | | | | | | | | | | | | | | | | | | 13 | | | | | |
| | | | | | | | | | | | | | | | | | | | | | | | | | 14 | | | | | |
| | | | | | | | | | | | | | | | | | | | | | | | | | 15 | | | | | |
| | | | | | | | | | | | | | | | | | | | | | | | | | 16 | | | | | |
| | | | | | | | | | | | | | | | | | | | | | | | | | 17 | | | | | |
| | | | | | | | | | | | | | | | | | | | | | | | | | 18 | | | | | |
| | | | | | | | | | | | | | | | | | | | | | | | | | 19 | | | | | |
| | | | | | | | | | | | | | | | | | | | | | | | | | 20 | | | | | |
| | | | | | | | | | | | | | | | | | | | | | | | | | 21 | | | | | |
| | | | | | | | | | | | | | | | | | | | | | | | | | 22 | | | | | |
| | | | | | | | | | | | | | | | | | | | | | | | | | 23 | | | | | |
| | | | | | | | | | | | | | | | | | | | | | | | | | 24 | | | | | |
| | | | | | | | | | | | | | | | | | | | | | | | | | 25 | | | | | |
| | | | | | | | | | | | | | | | | | | | | | | | | | 26 | | | | | |
| | | | | | | | | | | | | | | | | | | | | | | | | | 27 | | | | | |
| | | | | | | | | | | | | | | | | | | | | | | | | | 28 | | | | | |
| | | | | | | | | | | | | | | | | | | | | | | | | | 29 | | | | | |
| | | | | | | | | | | | | | | | | | | | | | | | | | 30 | | | | | |
| | | | | | | | | | | | | | | | | | | | | | | | | | 31 | | | | | |
| | | | | | | | | | | | | | | | | | | | | | | | | | 32 | | | | | |
| | | | | | | | | | | | | | | | | | | | | | | | | | 33 | | | | | |
| | | | | | | | | | | | | | | | | | | | | | | | | | 34 | | | | | |
| | | | | | | | | | | | | | | | | | | | | | | | | | 35 | | | | | |
| | | | | | | | | | | | | | | | | | | | | | | | | | 36 | | | | | |

# Subject _____

| Week | Week____ | | | | | Week____ | | | | | Week____ | | | | | Week____ | | | | | Week____ | | | |
|---|---|---|---|---|---|---|---|---|---|---|---|---|---|---|---|---|---|---|---|---|---|---|---|---|
| Day | M | T | W | T | F | M | T | W | T | F | M | T | W | T | F | M | T | W | T | F | M | T | W | T | F |
| Date | | | | | | | | | | | | | | | | | | | | | | | | | |
| Assignments or Attendance | | | | | | | | | | | | | | | | | | | | | | | | | |
| Name | | | | | | | | | | | | | | | | | | | | | | | | | |
| 1 | | | | | | | | | | | | | | | | | | | | | | | | | |
| 2 | | | | | | | | | | | | | | | | | | | | | | | | | |
| 3 | | | | | | | | | | | | | | | | | | | | | | | | | |
| 4 | | | | | | | | | | | | | | | | | | | | | | | | | |
| 5 | | | | | | | | | | | | | | | | | | | | | | | | | |
| 6 | | | | | | | | | | | | | | | | | | | | | | | | | |
| 7 | | | | | | | | | | | | | | | | | | | | | | | | | |
| 8 | | | | | | | | | | | | | | | | | | | | | | | | | |
| 9 | | | | | | | | | | | | | | | | | | | | | | | | | |
| 10 | | | | | | | | | | | | | | | | | | | | | | | | | |
| 11 | | | | | | | | | | | | | | | | | | | | | | | | | |
| 12 | | | | | | | | | | | | | | | | | | | | | | | | | |
| 13 | | | | | | | | | | | | | | | | | | | | | | | | | |
| 14 | | | | | | | | | | | | | | | | | | | | | | | | | |
| 15 | | | | | | | | | | | | | | | | | | | | | | | | | |
| 16 | | | | | | | | | | | | | | | | | | | | | | | | | |
| 17 | | | | | | | | | | | | | | | | | | | | | | | | | |
| 18 | | | | | | | | | | | | | | | | | | | | | | | | | |
| 19 | | | | | | | | | | | | | | | | | | | | | | | | | |
| 20 | | | | | | | | | | | | | | | | | | | | | | | | | |
| 21 | | | | | | | | | | | | | | | | | | | | | | | | | |
| 22 | | | | | | | | | | | | | | | | | | | | | | | | | |
| 23 | | | | | | | | | | | | | | | | | | | | | | | | | |
| 24 | | | | | | | | | | | | | | | | | | | | | | | | | |
| 25 | | | | | | | | | | | | | | | | | | | | | | | | | |
| 26 | | | | | | | | | | | | | | | | | | | | | | | | | |
| 27 | | | | | | | | | | | | | | | | | | | | | | | | | |
| 28 | | | | | | | | | | | | | | | | | | | | | | | | | |
| 29 | | | | | | | | | | | | | | | | | | | | | | | | | |
| 30 | | | | | | | | | | | | | | | | | | | | | | | | | |
| 31 | | | | | | | | | | | | | | | | | | | | | | | | | |
| 32 | | | | | | | | | | | | | | | | | | | | | | | | | |
| 33 | | | | | | | | | | | | | | | | | | | | | | | | | |
| 34 | | | | | | | | | | | | | | | | | | | | | | | | | |
| 35 | | | | | | | | | | | | | | | | | | | | | | | | | |
| 36 | | | | | | | | | | | | | | | | | | | | | | | | | |

# Period

| Week____ | Week____ | Week____ | Week____ | Week____ | | Days Present | Days Absent | Tardies | Quarter Grade | |
|---|---|---|---|---|---|---|---|---|---|---|
| M T W T F | M T W T F | M T W T F | M T W T F | M T W T F | | | | | | |
| | | | | | 1 | | | | | |
| | | | | | 2 | | | | | |
| | | | | | 3 | | | | | |
| | | | | | 4 | | | | | |
| | | | | | 5 | | | | | |
| | | | | | 6 | | | | | |
| | | | | | 7 | | | | | |
| | | | | | 8 | | | | | |
| | | | | | 9 | | | | | |
| | | | | | 10 | | | | | |
| | | | | | 11 | | | | | |
| | | | | | 12 | | | | | |
| | | | | | 13 | | | | | |
| | | | | | 14 | | | | | |
| | | | | | 15 | | | | | |
| | | | | | 16 | | | | | |
| | | | | | 17 | | | | | |
| | | | | | 18 | | | | | |
| | | | | | 19 | | | | | |
| | | | | | 20 | | | | | |
| | | | | | 21 | | | | | |
| | | | | | 22 | | | | | |
| | | | | | 23 | | | | | |
| | | | | | 24 | | | | | |
| | | | | | 25 | | | | | |
| | | | | | 26 | | | | | |
| | | | | | 27 | | | | | |
| | | | | | 28 | | | | | |
| | | | | | 29 | | | | | |
| | | | | | 30 | | | | | |
| | | | | | 31 | | | | | |
| | | | | | 32 | | | | | |
| | | | | | 33 | | | | | |
| | | | | | 34 | | | | | |
| | | | | | 35 | | | | | |
| | | | | | 36 | | | | | |

# Subject_____

| Week | Week____ | | | | | Week____ | | | | | Week____ | | | | | Week____ | | | | | Week____ | | | | |
|---|---|---|---|---|---|---|---|---|---|---|---|---|---|---|---|---|---|---|---|---|---|---|---|---|---|
| Day | M | T | W | T | F | M | T | W | T | F | M | T | W | T | F | M | T | W | T | F | M | T | W | T | F |
| Date | | | | | | | | | | | | | | | | | | | | | | | | | |
| Assignments or Attendance | | | | | | | | | | | | | | | | | | | | | | | | | |
| Name | | | | | | | | | | | | | | | | | | | | | | | | | |
| 1 | | | | | | | | | | | | | | | | | | | | | | | | | |
| 2 | | | | | | | | | | | | | | | | | | | | | | | | | |
| 3 | | | | | | | | | | | | | | | | | | | | | | | | | |
| 4 | | | | | | | | | | | | | | | | | | | | | | | | | |
| 5 | | | | | | | | | | | | | | | | | | | | | | | | | |
| 6 | | | | | | | | | | | | | | | | | | | | | | | | | |
| 7 | | | | | | | | | | | | | | | | | | | | | | | | | |
| 8 | | | | | | | | | | | | | | | | | | | | | | | | | |
| 9 | | | | | | | | | | | | | | | | | | | | | | | | | |
| 10 | | | | | | | | | | | | | | | | | | | | | | | | | |
| 11 | | | | | | | | | | | | | | | | | | | | | | | | | |
| 12 | | | | | | | | | | | | | | | | | | | | | | | | | |
| 13 | | | | | | | | | | | | | | | | | | | | | | | | | |
| 14 | | | | | | | | | | | | | | | | | | | | | | | | | |
| 15 | | | | | | | | | | | | | | | | | | | | | | | | | |
| 16 | | | | | | | | | | | | | | | | | | | | | | | | | |
| 17 | | | | | | | | | | | | | | | | | | | | | | | | | |
| 18 | | | | | | | | | | | | | | | | | | | | | | | | | |
| 19 | | | | | | | | | | | | | | | | | | | | | | | | | |
| 20 | | | | | | | | | | | | | | | | | | | | | | | | | |
| 21 | | | | | | | | | | | | | | | | | | | | | | | | | |
| 22 | | | | | | | | | | | | | | | | | | | | | | | | | |
| 23 | | | | | | | | | | | | | | | | | | | | | | | | | |
| 24 | | | | | | | | | | | | | | | | | | | | | | | | | |
| 25 | | | | | | | | | | | | | | | | | | | | | | | | | |
| 26 | | | | | | | | | | | | | | | | | | | | | | | | | |
| 27 | | | | | | | | | | | | | | | | | | | | | | | | | |
| 28 | | | | | | | | | | | | | | | | | | | | | | | | | |
| 29 | | | | | | | | | | | | | | | | | | | | | | | | | |
| 30 | | | | | | | | | | | | | | | | | | | | | | | | | |
| 31 | | | | | | | | | | | | | | | | | | | | | | | | | |
| 32 | | | | | | | | | | | | | | | | | | | | | | | | | |
| 33 | | | | | | | | | | | | | | | | | | | | | | | | | |
| 34 | | | | | | | | | | | | | | | | | | | | | | | | | |
| 35 | | | | | | | | | | | | | | | | | | | | | | | | | |
| 36 | | | | | | | | | | | | | | | | | | | | | | | | | |

# Period

| Week____ | | | | | Week____ | | | | | Week____ | | | | | Week____ | | | | | Week____ | | | | | | Days Present | Days Absent | Tardies | Quarter Grade | |
|---|---|---|---|---|---|---|---|---|---|---|---|---|---|---|---|---|---|---|---|---|---|---|---|---|---|---|---|---|---|---|
| M | T | W | T | F | M | T | W | T | F | M | T | W | T | F | M | T | W | T | F | M | T | W | T | F | | | | | | |
| | | | | | | | | | | | | | | | | | | | | | | | | | 1 | | | | | |
| | | | | | | | | | | | | | | | | | | | | | | | | | 2 | | | | | |
| | | | | | | | | | | | | | | | | | | | | | | | | | 3 | | | | | |
| | | | | | | | | | | | | | | | | | | | | | | | | | 4 | | | | | |
| | | | | | | | | | | | | | | | | | | | | | | | | | 5 | | | | | |
| | | | | | | | | | | | | | | | | | | | | | | | | | 6 | | | | | |
| | | | | | | | | | | | | | | | | | | | | | | | | | 7 | | | | | |
| | | | | | | | | | | | | | | | | | | | | | | | | | 8 | | | | | |
| | | | | | | | | | | | | | | | | | | | | | | | | | 9 | | | | | |
| | | | | | | | | | | | | | | | | | | | | | | | | | 10 | | | | | |
| | | | | | | | | | | | | | | | | | | | | | | | | | 11 | | | | | |
| | | | | | | | | | | | | | | | | | | | | | | | | | 12 | | | | | |
| | | | | | | | | | | | | | | | | | | | | | | | | | 13 | | | | | |
| | | | | | | | | | | | | | | | | | | | | | | | | | 14 | | | | | |
| | | | | | | | | | | | | | | | | | | | | | | | | | 15 | | | | | |
| | | | | | | | | | | | | | | | | | | | | | | | | | 16 | | | | | |
| | | | | | | | | | | | | | | | | | | | | | | | | | 17 | | | | | |
| | | | | | | | | | | | | | | | | | | | | | | | | | 18 | | | | | |
| | | | | | | | | | | | | | | | | | | | | | | | | | 19 | | | | | |
| | | | | | | | | | | | | | | | | | | | | | | | | | 20 | | | | | |
| | | | | | | | | | | | | | | | | | | | | | | | | | 21 | | | | | |
| | | | | | | | | | | | | | | | | | | | | | | | | | 22 | | | | | |
| | | | | | | | | | | | | | | | | | | | | | | | | | 23 | | | | | |
| | | | | | | | | | | | | | | | | | | | | | | | | | 24 | | | | | |
| | | | | | | | | | | | | | | | | | | | | | | | | | 25 | | | | | |
| | | | | | | | | | | | | | | | | | | | | | | | | | 26 | | | | | |
| | | | | | | | | | | | | | | | | | | | | | | | | | 27 | | | | | |
| | | | | | | | | | | | | | | | | | | | | | | | | | 28 | | | | | |
| | | | | | | | | | | | | | | | | | | | | | | | | | 29 | | | | | |
| | | | | | | | | | | | | | | | | | | | | | | | | | 30 | | | | | |
| | | | | | | | | | | | | | | | | | | | | | | | | | 31 | | | | | |
| | | | | | | | | | | | | | | | | | | | | | | | | | 32 | | | | | |
| | | | | | | | | | | | | | | | | | | | | | | | | | 33 | | | | | |
| | | | | | | | | | | | | | | | | | | | | | | | | | 34 | | | | | |
| | | | | | | | | | | | | | | | | | | | | | | | | | 35 | | | | | |
| | | | | | | | | | | | | | | | | | | | | | | | | | 36 | | | | | |

# Subject_____

| Week | Week____ | | | | Week____ | | | | Week____ | | | | Week____ | | | | Week____ | | | | Week____ | | | |
|---|---|---|---|---|---|---|---|---|---|---|---|---|---|---|---|---|---|---|---|---|---|---|---|---|
| Day | M | T | W | T | F | M | T | W | T | F | M | T | W | T | F | M | T | W | T | F | M | T | W | T | F |
| Date | | | | | | | | | | | | | | | | | | | | | | | | | |
| Assignments or Attendance | | | | | | | | | | | | | | | | | | | | | | | | | |
| Name | | | | | | | | | | | | | | | | | | | | | | | | | |
| 1 | | | | | | | | | | | | | | | | | | | | | | | | | |
| 2 | | | | | | | | | | | | | | | | | | | | | | | | | |
| 3 | | | | | | | | | | | | | | | | | | | | | | | | | |
| 4 | | | | | | | | | | | | | | | | | | | | | | | | | |
| 5 | | | | | | | | | | | | | | | | | | | | | | | | | |
| 6 | | | | | | | | | | | | | | | | | | | | | | | | | |
| 7 | | | | | | | | | | | | | | | | | | | | | | | | | |
| 8 | | | | | | | | | | | | | | | | | | | | | | | | | |
| 9 | | | | | | | | | | | | | | | | | | | | | | | | | |
| 10 | | | | | | | | | | | | | | | | | | | | | | | | | |
| 11 | | | | | | | | | | | | | | | | | | | | | | | | | |
| 12 | | | | | | | | | | | | | | | | | | | | | | | | | |
| 13 | | | | | | | | | | | | | | | | | | | | | | | | | |
| 14 | | | | | | | | | | | | | | | | | | | | | | | | | |
| 15 | | | | | | | | | | | | | | | | | | | | | | | | | |
| 16 | | | | | | | | | | | | | | | | | | | | | | | | | |
| 17 | | | | | | | | | | | | | | | | | | | | | | | | | |
| 18 | | | | | | | | | | | | | | | | | | | | | | | | | |
| 19 | | | | | | | | | | | | | | | | | | | | | | | | | |
| 20 | | | | | | | | | | | | | | | | | | | | | | | | | |
| 21 | | | | | | | | | | | | | | | | | | | | | | | | | |
| 22 | | | | | | | | | | | | | | | | | | | | | | | | | |
| 23 | | | | | | | | | | | | | | | | | | | | | | | | | |
| 24 | | | | | | | | | | | | | | | | | | | | | | | | | |
| 25 | | | | | | | | | | | | | | | | | | | | | | | | | |
| 26 | | | | | | | | | | | | | | | | | | | | | | | | | |
| 27 | | | | | | | | | | | | | | | | | | | | | | | | | |
| 28 | | | | | | | | | | | | | | | | | | | | | | | | | |
| 29 | | | | | | | | | | | | | | | | | | | | | | | | | |
| 30 | | | | | | | | | | | | | | | | | | | | | | | | | |
| 31 | | | | | | | | | | | | | | | | | | | | | | | | | |
| 32 | | | | | | | | | | | | | | | | | | | | | | | | | |
| 33 | | | | | | | | | | | | | | | | | | | | | | | | | |
| 34 | | | | | | | | | | | | | | | | | | | | | | | | | |
| 35 | | | | | | | | | | | | | | | | | | | | | | | | | |
| 36 | | | | | | | | | | | | | | | | | | | | | | | | | |

# Period _____

| Week____ | | | | | Week____ | | | | | Week____ | | | | | Week____ | | | | | Week____ | | | | | | Days Present | Days Absent | Tardies | Quarter Grade | |
|---|---|---|---|---|---|---|---|---|---|---|---|---|---|---|---|---|---|---|---|---|---|---|---|---|---|---|---|---|---|---|
| M | T | W | T | F | M | T | W | T | F | M | T | W | T | F | M | T | W | T | F | M | T | W | T | F | | | | | | |
| | | | | | | | | | | | | | | | | | | | | | | | | | | | | | | |
| | | | | | | | | | | | | | | | | | | | | | | | | | | | | | | |
| | | | | | | | | | | | | | | | | | | | | | | | | | 1 | | | | | |
| | | | | | | | | | | | | | | | | | | | | | | | | | 2 | | | | | |
| | | | | | | | | | | | | | | | | | | | | | | | | | 3 | | | | | |
| | | | | | | | | | | | | | | | | | | | | | | | | | 4 | | | | | |
| | | | | | | | | | | | | | | | | | | | | | | | | | 5 | | | | | |
| | | | | | | | | | | | | | | | | | | | | | | | | | 6 | | | | | |
| | | | | | | | | | | | | | | | | | | | | | | | | | 7 | | | | | |
| | | | | | | | | | | | | | | | | | | | | | | | | | 8 | | | | | |
| | | | | | | | | | | | | | | | | | | | | | | | | | 9 | | | | | |
| | | | | | | | | | | | | | | | | | | | | | | | | | 10 | | | | | |
| | | | | | | | | | | | | | | | | | | | | | | | | | 11 | | | | | |
| | | | | | | | | | | | | | | | | | | | | | | | | | 12 | | | | | |
| | | | | | | | | | | | | | | | | | | | | | | | | | 13 | | | | | |
| | | | | | | | | | | | | | | | | | | | | | | | | | 14 | | | | | |
| | | | | | | | | | | | | | | | | | | | | | | | | | 15 | | | | | |
| | | | | | | | | | | | | | | | | | | | | | | | | | 16 | | | | | |
| | | | | | | | | | | | | | | | | | | | | | | | | | 17 | | | | | |
| | | | | | | | | | | | | | | | | | | | | | | | | | 18 | | | | | |
| | | | | | | | | | | | | | | | | | | | | | | | | | 19 | | | | | |
| | | | | | | | | | | | | | | | | | | | | | | | | | 20 | | | | | |
| | | | | | | | | | | | | | | | | | | | | | | | | | 21 | | | | | |
| | | | | | | | | | | | | | | | | | | | | | | | | | 22 | | | | | |
| | | | | | | | | | | | | | | | | | | | | | | | | | 23 | | | | | |
| | | | | | | | | | | | | | | | | | | | | | | | | | 24 | | | | | |
| | | | | | | | | | | | | | | | | | | | | | | | | | 25 | | | | | |
| | | | | | | | | | | | | | | | | | | | | | | | | | 26 | | | | | |
| | | | | | | | | | | | | | | | | | | | | | | | | | 27 | | | | | |
| | | | | | | | | | | | | | | | | | | | | | | | | | 28 | | | | | |
| | | | | | | | | | | | | | | | | | | | | | | | | | 29 | | | | | |
| | | | | | | | | | | | | | | | | | | | | | | | | | 30 | | | | | |
| | | | | | | | | | | | | | | | | | | | | | | | | | 31 | | | | | |
| | | | | | | | | | | | | | | | | | | | | | | | | | 32 | | | | | |
| | | | | | | | | | | | | | | | | | | | | | | | | | 33 | | | | | |
| | | | | | | | | | | | | | | | | | | | | | | | | | 34 | | | | | |
| | | | | | | | | | | | | | | | | | | | | | | | | | 35 | | | | | |
| | | | | | | | | | | | | | | | | | | | | | | | | | 36 | | | | | |

# Subject_____

| Week | Week____ | | | | | Week____ | | | | | Week____ | | | | | Week____ | | | | | Week____ | | | | |
|---|---|---|---|---|---|---|---|---|---|---|---|---|---|---|---|---|---|---|---|---|---|---|---|---|---|
| Day | M | T | W | T | F | M | T | W | T | F | M | T | W | T | F | M | T | W | T | F | M | T | W | T | F |
| Date | | | | | | | | | | | | | | | | | | | | | | | | | |
| Assignments or Attendance | | | | | | | | | | | | | | | | | | | | | | | | | |
| Name | | | | | | | | | | | | | | | | | | | | | | | | | |
| 1 | | | | | | | | | | | | | | | | | | | | | | | | | |
| 2 | | | | | | | | | | | | | | | | | | | | | | | | | |
| 3 | | | | | | | | | | | | | | | | | | | | | | | | | |
| 4 | | | | | | | | | | | | | | | | | | | | | | | | | |
| 5 | | | | | | | | | | | | | | | | | | | | | | | | | |
| 6 | | | | | | | | | | | | | | | | | | | | | | | | | |
| 7 | | | | | | | | | | | | | | | | | | | | | | | | | |
| 8 | | | | | | | | | | | | | | | | | | | | | | | | | |
| 9 | | | | | | | | | | | | | | | | | | | | | | | | | |
| 10 | | | | | | | | | | | | | | | | | | | | | | | | | |
| 11 | | | | | | | | | | | | | | | | | | | | | | | | | |
| 12 | | | | | | | | | | | | | | | | | | | | | | | | | |
| 13 | | | | | | | | | | | | | | | | | | | | | | | | | |
| 14 | | | | | | | | | | | | | | | | | | | | | | | | | |
| 15 | | | | | | | | | | | | | | | | | | | | | | | | | |
| 16 | | | | | | | | | | | | | | | | | | | | | | | | | |
| 17 | | | | | | | | | | | | | | | | | | | | | | | | | |
| 18 | | | | | | | | | | | | | | | | | | | | | | | | | |
| 19 | | | | | | | | | | | | | | | | | | | | | | | | | |
| 20 | | | | | | | | | | | | | | | | | | | | | | | | | |
| 21 | | | | | | | | | | | | | | | | | | | | | | | | | |
| 22 | | | | | | | | | | | | | | | | | | | | | | | | | |
| 23 | | | | | | | | | | | | | | | | | | | | | | | | | |
| 24 | | | | | | | | | | | | | | | | | | | | | | | | | |
| 25 | | | | | | | | | | | | | | | | | | | | | | | | | |
| 26 | | | | | | | | | | | | | | | | | | | | | | | | | |
| 27 | | | | | | | | | | | | | | | | | | | | | | | | | |
| 28 | | | | | | | | | | | | | | | | | | | | | | | | | |
| 29 | | | | | | | | | | | | | | | | | | | | | | | | | |
| 30 | | | | | | | | | | | | | | | | | | | | | | | | | |
| 31 | | | | | | | | | | | | | | | | | | | | | | | | | |
| 32 | | | | | | | | | | | | | | | | | | | | | | | | | |
| 33 | | | | | | | | | | | | | | | | | | | | | | | | | |
| 34 | | | | | | | | | | | | | | | | | | | | | | | | | |
| 35 | | | | | | | | | | | | | | | | | | | | | | | | | |
| 36 | | | | | | | | | | | | | | | | | | | | | | | | | |

# Period_____

| Week____ | | | | | Week____ | | | | | Week____ | | | | | Week____ | | | | | Week____ | | | | | | Days Present | Days Absent | Tardies | Quarter Grade | |
|---|---|---|---|---|---|---|---|---|---|---|---|---|---|---|---|---|---|---|---|---|---|---|---|---|---|---|---|---|---|---|
| M | T | W | T | F | M | T | W | T | F | M | T | W | T | F | M | T | W | T | F | M | T | W | T | F | | | | | | |
| | | | | | | | | | | | | | | | | | | | | | | | | | | | | | | |
| | | | | | | | | | | | | | | | | | | | | | | | | | | | | | | |
| | | | | | | | | | | | | | | | | | | | | | | | | | 1 | | | | | |
| | | | | | | | | | | | | | | | | | | | | | | | | | 2 | | | | | |
| | | | | | | | | | | | | | | | | | | | | | | | | | 3 | | | | | |
| | | | | | | | | | | | | | | | | | | | | | | | | | 4 | | | | | |
| | | | | | | | | | | | | | | | | | | | | | | | | | 5 | | | | | |
| | | | | | | | | | | | | | | | | | | | | | | | | | 6 | | | | | |
| | | | | | | | | | | | | | | | | | | | | | | | | | 7 | | | | | |
| | | | | | | | | | | | | | | | | | | | | | | | | | 8 | | | | | |
| | | | | | | | | | | | | | | | | | | | | | | | | | 9 | | | | | |
| | | | | | | | | | | | | | | | | | | | | | | | | | 10 | | | | | |
| | | | | | | | | | | | | | | | | | | | | | | | | | 11 | | | | | |
| | | | | | | | | | | | | | | | | | | | | | | | | | 12 | | | | | |
| | | | | | | | | | | | | | | | | | | | | | | | | | 13 | | | | | |
| | | | | | | | | | | | | | | | | | | | | | | | | | 14 | | | | | |
| | | | | | | | | | | | | | | | | | | | | | | | | | 15 | | | | | |
| | | | | | | | | | | | | | | | | | | | | | | | | | 16 | | | | | |
| | | | | | | | | | | | | | | | | | | | | | | | | | 17 | | | | | |
| | | | | | | | | | | | | | | | | | | | | | | | | | 18 | | | | | |
| | | | | | | | | | | | | | | | | | | | | | | | | | 19 | | | | | |
| | | | | | | | | | | | | | | | | | | | | | | | | | 20 | | | | | |
| | | | | | | | | | | | | | | | | | | | | | | | | | 21 | | | | | |
| | | | | | | | | | | | | | | | | | | | | | | | | | 22 | | | | | |
| | | | | | | | | | | | | | | | | | | | | | | | | | 23 | | | | | |
| | | | | | | | | | | | | | | | | | | | | | | | | | 24 | | | | | |
| | | | | | | | | | | | | | | | | | | | | | | | | | 25 | | | | | |
| | | | | | | | | | | | | | | | | | | | | | | | | | 26 | | | | | |
| | | | | | | | | | | | | | | | | | | | | | | | | | 27 | | | | | |
| | | | | | | | | | | | | | | | | | | | | | | | | | 28 | | | | | |
| | | | | | | | | | | | | | | | | | | | | | | | | | 29 | | | | | |
| | | | | | | | | | | | | | | | | | | | | | | | | | 30 | | | | | |
| | | | | | | | | | | | | | | | | | | | | | | | | | 31 | | | | | |
| | | | | | | | | | | | | | | | | | | | | | | | | | 32 | | | | | |
| | | | | | | | | | | | | | | | | | | | | | | | | | 33 | | | | | |
| | | | | | | | | | | | | | | | | | | | | | | | | | 34 | | | | | |
| | | | | | | | | | | | | | | | | | | | | | | | | | 35 | | | | | |
| | | | | | | | | | | | | | | | | | | | | | | | | | 36 | | | | | |

# Subject_____

| Week | Week____ | | | | Week____ | | | | Week____ | | | | Week____ | | | | Week____ | | | | Week____ | | | |
|---|---|---|---|---|---|---|---|---|---|---|---|---|---|---|---|---|---|---|---|---|---|---|---|---|
| Day | M | T | W | T | F | M | T | W | T | F | M | T | W | T | F | M | T | W | T | F | M | T | W | T | F |
| Date | | | | | | | | | | | | | | | | | | | | | | | | | |
| Assignments or Attendance | | | | | | | | | | | | | | | | | | | | | | | | | |
| Name | | | | | | | | | | | | | | | | | | | | | | | | | |
| 1 | | | | | | | | | | | | | | | | | | | | | | | | | |
| 2 | | | | | | | | | | | | | | | | | | | | | | | | | |
| 3 | | | | | | | | | | | | | | | | | | | | | | | | | |
| 4 | | | | | | | | | | | | | | | | | | | | | | | | | |
| 5 | | | | | | | | | | | | | | | | | | | | | | | | | |
| 6 | | | | | | | | | | | | | | | | | | | | | | | | | |
| 7 | | | | | | | | | | | | | | | | | | | | | | | | | |
| 8 | | | | | | | | | | | | | | | | | | | | | | | | | |
| 9 | | | | | | | | | | | | | | | | | | | | | | | | | |
| 10 | | | | | | | | | | | | | | | | | | | | | | | | | |
| 11 | | | | | | | | | | | | | | | | | | | | | | | | | |
| 12 | | | | | | | | | | | | | | | | | | | | | | | | | |
| 13 | | | | | | | | | | | | | | | | | | | | | | | | | |
| 14 | | | | | | | | | | | | | | | | | | | | | | | | | |
| 15 | | | | | | | | | | | | | | | | | | | | | | | | | |
| 16 | | | | | | | | | | | | | | | | | | | | | | | | | |
| 17 | | | | | | | | | | | | | | | | | | | | | | | | | |
| 18 | | | | | | | | | | | | | | | | | | | | | | | | | |
| 19 | | | | | | | | | | | | | | | | | | | | | | | | | |
| 20 | | | | | | | | | | | | | | | | | | | | | | | | | |
| 21 | | | | | | | | | | | | | | | | | | | | | | | | | |
| 22 | | | | | | | | | | | | | | | | | | | | | | | | | |
| 23 | | | | | | | | | | | | | | | | | | | | | | | | | |
| 24 | | | | | | | | | | | | | | | | | | | | | | | | | |
| 25 | | | | | | | | | | | | | | | | | | | | | | | | | |
| 26 | | | | | | | | | | | | | | | | | | | | | | | | | |
| 27 | | | | | | | | | | | | | | | | | | | | | | | | | |
| 28 | | | | | | | | | | | | | | | | | | | | | | | | | |
| 29 | | | | | | | | | | | | | | | | | | | | | | | | | |
| 30 | | | | | | | | | | | | | | | | | | | | | | | | | |
| 31 | | | | | | | | | | | | | | | | | | | | | | | | | |
| 32 | | | | | | | | | | | | | | | | | | | | | | | | | |
| 33 | | | | | | | | | | | | | | | | | | | | | | | | | |
| 34 | | | | | | | | | | | | | | | | | | | | | | | | | |
| 35 | | | | | | | | | | | | | | | | | | | | | | | | | |
| 36 | | | | | | | | | | | | | | | | | | | | | | | | | |

# Period_____

| Week____ | Week____ | Week____ | Week____ | Week____ | | Days Present | Days Absent | Tardies | Quarter Grade | | |
|---|---|---|---|---|---|---|---|---|---|---|---|
| M T W T F | M T W T F | M T W T F | M T W T F | M T W T F | | | | | | | |
| | | | | | | | | | | | |
| | | | | | | | | | | | |
| | | | | | | | | | | | |
| | | | | | 1 | | | | | | |
| | | | | | 2 | | | | | | |
| | | | | | 3 | | | | | | |
| | | | | | 4 | | | | | | |
| | | | | | 5 | | | | | | |
| | | | | | 6 | | | | | | |
| | | | | | 7 | | | | | | |
| | | | | | 8 | | | | | | |
| | | | | | 9 | | | | | | |
| | | | | | 10 | | | | | | |
| | | | | | 11 | | | | | | |
| | | | | | 12 | | | | | | |
| | | | | | 13 | | | | | | |
| | | | | | 14 | | | | | | |
| | | | | | 15 | | | | | | |
| | | | | | 16 | | | | | | |
| | | | | | 17 | | | | | | |
| | | | | | 18 | | | | | | |
| | | | | | 19 | | | | | | |
| | | | | | 20 | | | | | | |
| | | | | | 21 | | | | | | |
| | | | | | 22 | | | | | | |
| | | | | | 23 | | | | | | |
| | | | | | 24 | | | | | | |
| | | | | | 25 | | | | | | |
| | | | | | 26 | | | | | | |
| | | | | | 27 | | | | | | |
| | | | | | 28 | | | | | | |
| | | | | | 29 | | | | | | |
| | | | | | 30 | | | | | | |
| | | | | | 31 | | | | | | |
| | | | | | 32 | | | | | | |
| | | | | | 33 | | | | | | |
| | | | | | 34 | | | | | | |
| | | | | | 35 | | | | | | |
| | | | | | 36 | | | | | | |

# Subject_____

| Week | Week____ | | | | | Week____ | | | | | Week____ | | | | | Week____ | | | | | Week____ | | | | |
|---|---|---|---|---|---|---|---|---|---|---|---|---|---|---|---|---|---|---|---|---|---|---|---|---|---|
| Day | M | T | W | T | F | M | T | W | T | F | M | T | W | T | F | M | T | W | T | F | M | T | W | T | F |
| Date | | | | | | | | | | | | | | | | | | | | | | | | | |
| Assignments or Attendance | | | | | | | | | | | | | | | | | | | | | | | | | |
| Name | | | | | | | | | | | | | | | | | | | | | | | | | |
| 1 | | | | | | | | | | | | | | | | | | | | | | | | | |
| 2 | | | | | | | | | | | | | | | | | | | | | | | | | |
| 3 | | | | | | | | | | | | | | | | | | | | | | | | | |
| 4 | | | | | | | | | | | | | | | | | | | | | | | | | |
| 5 | | | | | | | | | | | | | | | | | | | | | | | | | |
| 6 | | | | | | | | | | | | | | | | | | | | | | | | | |
| 7 | | | | | | | | | | | | | | | | | | | | | | | | | |
| 8 | | | | | | | | | | | | | | | | | | | | | | | | | |
| 9 | | | | | | | | | | | | | | | | | | | | | | | | | |
| 10 | | | | | | | | | | | | | | | | | | | | | | | | | |
| 11 | | | | | | | | | | | | | | | | | | | | | | | | | |
| 12 | | | | | | | | | | | | | | | | | | | | | | | | | |
| 13 | | | | | | | | | | | | | | | | | | | | | | | | | |
| 14 | | | | | | | | | | | | | | | | | | | | | | | | | |
| 15 | | | | | | | | | | | | | | | | | | | | | | | | | |
| 16 | | | | | | | | | | | | | | | | | | | | | | | | | |
| 17 | | | | | | | | | | | | | | | | | | | | | | | | | |
| 18 | | | | | | | | | | | | | | | | | | | | | | | | | |
| 19 | | | | | | | | | | | | | | | | | | | | | | | | | |
| 20 | | | | | | | | | | | | | | | | | | | | | | | | | |
| 21 | | | | | | | | | | | | | | | | | | | | | | | | | |
| 22 | | | | | | | | | | | | | | | | | | | | | | | | | |
| 23 | | | | | | | | | | | | | | | | | | | | | | | | | |
| 24 | | | | | | | | | | | | | | | | | | | | | | | | | |
| 25 | | | | | | | | | | | | | | | | | | | | | | | | | |
| 26 | | | | | | | | | | | | | | | | | | | | | | | | | |
| 27 | | | | | | | | | | | | | | | | | | | | | | | | | |
| 28 | | | | | | | | | | | | | | | | | | | | | | | | | |
| 29 | | | | | | | | | | | | | | | | | | | | | | | | | |
| 30 | | | | | | | | | | | | | | | | | | | | | | | | | |
| 31 | | | | | | | | | | | | | | | | | | | | | | | | | |
| 32 | | | | | | | | | | | | | | | | | | | | | | | | | |
| 33 | | | | | | | | | | | | | | | | | | | | | | | | | |
| 34 | | | | | | | | | | | | | | | | | | | | | | | | | |
| 35 | | | | | | | | | | | | | | | | | | | | | | | | | |
| 36 | | | | | | | | | | | | | | | | | | | | | | | | | |

# Period

| Week____ | | | | | Week____ | | | | | Week____ | | | | | Week____ | | | | | Week____ | | | | | | Days Present | Days Absent | Tardies | Quarter Grade | | |
|---|---|---|---|---|---|---|---|---|---|---|---|---|---|---|---|---|---|---|---|---|---|---|---|---|---|---|---|---|---|---|---|
| M | T | W | T | F | M | T | W | T | F | M | T | W | T | F | M | T | W | T | F | M | T | W | T | F | | | | | | | |
| | | | | | | | | | | | | | | | | | | | | | | | | | | | | | | | |
| | | | | | | | | | | | | | | | | | | | | | | | | | | | | | | | |
| | | | | | | | | | | | | | | | | | | | | | | | | | 1 | | | | | | |
| | | | | | | | | | | | | | | | | | | | | | | | | | 2 | | | | | | |
| | | | | | | | | | | | | | | | | | | | | | | | | | 3 | | | | | | |
| | | | | | | | | | | | | | | | | | | | | | | | | | 4 | | | | | | |
| | | | | | | | | | | | | | | | | | | | | | | | | | 5 | | | | | | |
| | | | | | | | | | | | | | | | | | | | | | | | | | 6 | | | | | | |
| | | | | | | | | | | | | | | | | | | | | | | | | | 7 | | | | | | |
| | | | | | | | | | | | | | | | | | | | | | | | | | 8 | | | | | | |
| | | | | | | | | | | | | | | | | | | | | | | | | | 9 | | | | | | |
| | | | | | | | | | | | | | | | | | | | | | | | | | 10 | | | | | | |
| | | | | | | | | | | | | | | | | | | | | | | | | | 11 | | | | | | |
| | | | | | | | | | | | | | | | | | | | | | | | | | 12 | | | | | | |
| | | | | | | | | | | | | | | | | | | | | | | | | | 13 | | | | | | |
| | | | | | | | | | | | | | | | | | | | | | | | | | 14 | | | | | | |
| | | | | | | | | | | | | | | | | | | | | | | | | | 15 | | | | | | |
| | | | | | | | | | | | | | | | | | | | | | | | | | 16 | | | | | | |
| | | | | | | | | | | | | | | | | | | | | | | | | | 17 | | | | | | |
| | | | | | | | | | | | | | | | | | | | | | | | | | 18 | | | | | | |
| | | | | | | | | | | | | | | | | | | | | | | | | | 19 | | | | | | |
| | | | | | | | | | | | | | | | | | | | | | | | | | 20 | | | | | | |
| | | | | | | | | | | | | | | | | | | | | | | | | | 21 | | | | | | |
| | | | | | | | | | | | | | | | | | | | | | | | | | 22 | | | | | | |
| | | | | | | | | | | | | | | | | | | | | | | | | | 23 | | | | | | |
| | | | | | | | | | | | | | | | | | | | | | | | | | 24 | | | | | | |
| | | | | | | | | | | | | | | | | | | | | | | | | | 25 | | | | | | |
| | | | | | | | | | | | | | | | | | | | | | | | | | 26 | | | | | | |
| | | | | | | | | | | | | | | | | | | | | | | | | | 27 | | | | | | |
| | | | | | | | | | | | | | | | | | | | | | | | | | 28 | | | | | | |
| | | | | | | | | | | | | | | | | | | | | | | | | | 29 | | | | | | |
| | | | | | | | | | | | | | | | | | | | | | | | | | 30 | | | | | | |
| | | | | | | | | | | | | | | | | | | | | | | | | | 31 | | | | | | |
| | | | | | | | | | | | | | | | | | | | | | | | | | 32 | | | | | | |
| | | | | | | | | | | | | | | | | | | | | | | | | | 33 | | | | | | |
| | | | | | | | | | | | | | | | | | | | | | | | | | 34 | | | | | | |
| | | | | | | | | | | | | | | | | | | | | | | | | | 35 | | | | | | |
| | | | | | | | | | | | | | | | | | | | | | | | | | 36 | | | | | | |

# Subject_____

| Week | Week____ | | | | | Week____ | | | | | Week____ | | | | | Week____ | | | | | Week____ | | | | |
|---|---|---|---|---|---|---|---|---|---|---|---|---|---|---|---|---|---|---|---|---|---|---|---|---|---|
| Day | M | T | W | T | F | M | T | W | T | F | M | T | W | T | F | M | T | W | T | F | M | T | W | T | F |
| Date | | | | | | | | | | | | | | | | | | | | | | | | | |
| Assignments or Attendance | | | | | | | | | | | | | | | | | | | | | | | | | |
| Name | | | | | | | | | | | | | | | | | | | | | | | | | |
| 1 | | | | | | | | | | | | | | | | | | | | | | | | | |
| 2 | | | | | | | | | | | | | | | | | | | | | | | | | |
| 3 | | | | | | | | | | | | | | | | | | | | | | | | | |
| 4 | | | | | | | | | | | | | | | | | | | | | | | | | |
| 5 | | | | | | | | | | | | | | | | | | | | | | | | | |
| 6 | | | | | | | | | | | | | | | | | | | | | | | | | |
| 7 | | | | | | | | | | | | | | | | | | | | | | | | | |
| 8 | | | | | | | | | | | | | | | | | | | | | | | | | |
| 9 | | | | | | | | | | | | | | | | | | | | | | | | | |
| 10 | | | | | | | | | | | | | | | | | | | | | | | | | |
| 11 | | | | | | | | | | | | | | | | | | | | | | | | | |
| 12 | | | | | | | | | | | | | | | | | | | | | | | | | |
| 13 | | | | | | | | | | | | | | | | | | | | | | | | | |
| 14 | | | | | | | | | | | | | | | | | | | | | | | | | |
| 15 | | | | | | | | | | | | | | | | | | | | | | | | | |
| 16 | | | | | | | | | | | | | | | | | | | | | | | | | |
| 17 | | | | | | | | | | | | | | | | | | | | | | | | | |
| 18 | | | | | | | | | | | | | | | | | | | | | | | | | |
| 19 | | | | | | | | | | | | | | | | | | | | | | | | | |
| 20 | | | | | | | | | | | | | | | | | | | | | | | | | |
| 21 | | | | | | | | | | | | | | | | | | | | | | | | | |
| 22 | | | | | | | | | | | | | | | | | | | | | | | | | |
| 23 | | | | | | | | | | | | | | | | | | | | | | | | | |
| 24 | | | | | | | | | | | | | | | | | | | | | | | | | |
| 25 | | | | | | | | | | | | | | | | | | | | | | | | | |
| 26 | | | | | | | | | | | | | | | | | | | | | | | | | |
| 27 | | | | | | | | | | | | | | | | | | | | | | | | | |
| 28 | | | | | | | | | | | | | | | | | | | | | | | | | |
| 29 | | | | | | | | | | | | | | | | | | | | | | | | | |
| 30 | | | | | | | | | | | | | | | | | | | | | | | | | |
| 31 | | | | | | | | | | | | | | | | | | | | | | | | | |
| 32 | | | | | | | | | | | | | | | | | | | | | | | | | |
| 33 | | | | | | | | | | | | | | | | | | | | | | | | | |
| 34 | | | | | | | | | | | | | | | | | | | | | | | | | |
| 35 | | | | | | | | | | | | | | | | | | | | | | | | | |
| 36 | | | | | | | | | | | | | | | | | | | | | | | | | |

# Period _____

| Week____ |||| Week____ |||| Week____ |||| Week____ |||| Week____ |||| | Days Present | Days Absent | Tardies | Quarter Grade | |
|M|T|W|T|F|M|T|W|T|F|M|T|W|T|F|M|T|W|T|F|M|T|W|T|F| | | | | | |
| | | | | | | | | | | | | | | | | | | | | | | | | | 1 | | | | | |
| | | | | | | | | | | | | | | | | | | | | | | | | | 2 | | | | | |
| | | | | | | | | | | | | | | | | | | | | | | | | | 3 | | | | | |
| | | | | | | | | | | | | | | | | | | | | | | | | | 4 | | | | | |
| | | | | | | | | | | | | | | | | | | | | | | | | | 5 | | | | | |
| | | | | | | | | | | | | | | | | | | | | | | | | | 6 | | | | | |
| | | | | | | | | | | | | | | | | | | | | | | | | | 7 | | | | | |
| | | | | | | | | | | | | | | | | | | | | | | | | | 8 | | | | | |
| | | | | | | | | | | | | | | | | | | | | | | | | | 9 | | | | | |
| | | | | | | | | | | | | | | | | | | | | | | | | | 10 | | | | | |
| | | | | | | | | | | | | | | | | | | | | | | | | | 11 | | | | | |
| | | | | | | | | | | | | | | | | | | | | | | | | | 12 | | | | | |
| | | | | | | | | | | | | | | | | | | | | | | | | | 13 | | | | | |
| | | | | | | | | | | | | | | | | | | | | | | | | | 14 | | | | | |
| | | | | | | | | | | | | | | | | | | | | | | | | | 15 | | | | | |
| | | | | | | | | | | | | | | | | | | | | | | | | | 16 | | | | | |
| | | | | | | | | | | | | | | | | | | | | | | | | | 17 | | | | | |
| | | | | | | | | | | | | | | | | | | | | | | | | | 18 | | | | | |
| | | | | | | | | | | | | | | | | | | | | | | | | | 19 | | | | | |
| | | | | | | | | | | | | | | | | | | | | | | | | | 20 | | | | | |
| | | | | | | | | | | | | | | | | | | | | | | | | | 21 | | | | | |
| | | | | | | | | | | | | | | | | | | | | | | | | | 22 | | | | | |
| | | | | | | | | | | | | | | | | | | | | | | | | | 23 | | | | | |
| | | | | | | | | | | | | | | | | | | | | | | | | | 24 | | | | | |
| | | | | | | | | | | | | | | | | | | | | | | | | | 25 | | | | | |
| | | | | | | | | | | | | | | | | | | | | | | | | | 26 | | | | | |
| | | | | | | | | | | | | | | | | | | | | | | | | | 27 | | | | | |
| | | | | | | | | | | | | | | | | | | | | | | | | | 28 | | | | | |
| | | | | | | | | | | | | | | | | | | | | | | | | | 29 | | | | | |
| | | | | | | | | | | | | | | | | | | | | | | | | | 30 | | | | | |
| | | | | | | | | | | | | | | | | | | | | | | | | | 31 | | | | | |
| | | | | | | | | | | | | | | | | | | | | | | | | | 32 | | | | | |
| | | | | | | | | | | | | | | | | | | | | | | | | | 33 | | | | | |
| | | | | | | | | | | | | | | | | | | | | | | | | | 34 | | | | | |
| | | | | | | | | | | | | | | | | | | | | | | | | | 35 | | | | | |
| | | | | | | | | | | | | | | | | | | | | | | | | | 36 | | | | | |

# Subject_____

| Week | Week____ | | | | | Week____ | | | | | Week____ | | | | | Week____ | | | | | Week____ | | | | | Week____ | | | | |
|---|---|---|---|---|---|---|---|---|---|---|---|---|---|---|---|---|---|---|---|---|---|---|---|---|---|---|---|---|---|---|
| Day | M | T | W | T | F | M | T | W | T | F | M | T | W | T | F | M | T | W | T | F | M | T | W | T | F | M | T | W | T | F |
| Date | | | | | | | | | | | | | | | | | | | | | | | | | | | | | | |
| Assignments or Attendance | | | | | | | | | | | | | | | | | | | | | | | | | | | | | | |
| Name | | | | | | | | | | | | | | | | | | | | | | | | | | | | | | |
| 1 | | | | | | | | | | | | | | | | | | | | | | | | | | | | | | |
| 2 | | | | | | | | | | | | | | | | | | | | | | | | | | | | | | |
| 3 | | | | | | | | | | | | | | | | | | | | | | | | | | | | | | |
| 4 | | | | | | | | | | | | | | | | | | | | | | | | | | | | | | |
| 5 | | | | | | | | | | | | | | | | | | | | | | | | | | | | | | |
| 6 | | | | | | | | | | | | | | | | | | | | | | | | | | | | | | |
| 7 | | | | | | | | | | | | | | | | | | | | | | | | | | | | | | |
| 8 | | | | | | | | | | | | | | | | | | | | | | | | | | | | | | |
| 9 | | | | | | | | | | | | | | | | | | | | | | | | | | | | | | |
| 10 | | | | | | | | | | | | | | | | | | | | | | | | | | | | | | |
| 11 | | | | | | | | | | | | | | | | | | | | | | | | | | | | | | |
| 12 | | | | | | | | | | | | | | | | | | | | | | | | | | | | | | |
| 13 | | | | | | | | | | | | | | | | | | | | | | | | | | | | | | |
| 14 | | | | | | | | | | | | | | | | | | | | | | | | | | | | | | |
| 15 | | | | | | | | | | | | | | | | | | | | | | | | | | | | | | |
| 16 | | | | | | | | | | | | | | | | | | | | | | | | | | | | | | |
| 17 | | | | | | | | | | | | | | | | | | | | | | | | | | | | | | |
| 18 | | | | | | | | | | | | | | | | | | | | | | | | | | | | | | |
| 19 | | | | | | | | | | | | | | | | | | | | | | | | | | | | | | |
| 20 | | | | | | | | | | | | | | | | | | | | | | | | | | | | | | |
| 21 | | | | | | | | | | | | | | | | | | | | | | | | | | | | | | |
| 22 | | | | | | | | | | | | | | | | | | | | | | | | | | | | | | |
| 23 | | | | | | | | | | | | | | | | | | | | | | | | | | | | | | |
| 24 | | | | | | | | | | | | | | | | | | | | | | | | | | | | | | |
| 25 | | | | | | | | | | | | | | | | | | | | | | | | | | | | | | |
| 26 | | | | | | | | | | | | | | | | | | | | | | | | | | | | | | |
| 27 | | | | | | | | | | | | | | | | | | | | | | | | | | | | | | |
| 28 | | | | | | | | | | | | | | | | | | | | | | | | | | | | | | |
| 29 | | | | | | | | | | | | | | | | | | | | | | | | | | | | | | |
| 30 | | | | | | | | | | | | | | | | | | | | | | | | | | | | | | |
| 31 | | | | | | | | | | | | | | | | | | | | | | | | | | | | | | |
| 32 | | | | | | | | | | | | | | | | | | | | | | | | | | | | | | |
| 33 | | | | | | | | | | | | | | | | | | | | | | | | | | | | | | |
| 34 | | | | | | | | | | | | | | | | | | | | | | | | | | | | | | |
| 35 | | | | | | | | | | | | | | | | | | | | | | | | | | | | | | |
| 36 | | | | | | | | | | | | | | | | | | | | | | | | | | | | | | |

# Period _____

| Week____ | | | | | Week____ | | | | | Week____ | | | | | Week____ | | | | | Week____ | | | | | | Days Present | Days Absent | Tardies | Quarter Grade | | |
|---|---|---|---|---|---|---|---|---|---|---|---|---|---|---|---|---|---|---|---|---|---|---|---|---|---|---|---|---|---|---|
| M | T | W | T | F | M | T | W | T | F | M | T | W | T | F | M | T | W | T | F | M | T | W | T | F | | | | | | |
| | | | | | | | | | | | | | | | | | | | | | | | | | 1 | | | | | |
| | | | | | | | | | | | | | | | | | | | | | | | | | 2 | | | | | |
| | | | | | | | | | | | | | | | | | | | | | | | | | 3 | | | | | |
| | | | | | | | | | | | | | | | | | | | | | | | | | 4 | | | | | |
| | | | | | | | | | | | | | | | | | | | | | | | | | 5 | | | | | |
| | | | | | | | | | | | | | | | | | | | | | | | | | 6 | | | | | |
| | | | | | | | | | | | | | | | | | | | | | | | | | 7 | | | | | |
| | | | | | | | | | | | | | | | | | | | | | | | | | 8 | | | | | |
| | | | | | | | | | | | | | | | | | | | | | | | | | 9 | | | | | |
| | | | | | | | | | | | | | | | | | | | | | | | | | 10 | | | | | |
| | | | | | | | | | | | | | | | | | | | | | | | | | 11 | | | | | |
| | | | | | | | | | | | | | | | | | | | | | | | | | 12 | | | | | |
| | | | | | | | | | | | | | | | | | | | | | | | | | 13 | | | | | |
| | | | | | | | | | | | | | | | | | | | | | | | | | 14 | | | | | |
| | | | | | | | | | | | | | | | | | | | | | | | | | 15 | | | | | |
| | | | | | | | | | | | | | | | | | | | | | | | | | 16 | | | | | |
| | | | | | | | | | | | | | | | | | | | | | | | | | 17 | | | | | |
| | | | | | | | | | | | | | | | | | | | | | | | | | 18 | | | | | |
| | | | | | | | | | | | | | | | | | | | | | | | | | 19 | | | | | |
| | | | | | | | | | | | | | | | | | | | | | | | | | 20 | | | | | |
| | | | | | | | | | | | | | | | | | | | | | | | | | 21 | | | | | |
| | | | | | | | | | | | | | | | | | | | | | | | | | 22 | | | | | |
| | | | | | | | | | | | | | | | | | | | | | | | | | 23 | | | | | |
| | | | | | | | | | | | | | | | | | | | | | | | | | 24 | | | | | |
| | | | | | | | | | | | | | | | | | | | | | | | | | 25 | | | | | |
| | | | | | | | | | | | | | | | | | | | | | | | | | 26 | | | | | |
| | | | | | | | | | | | | | | | | | | | | | | | | | 27 | | | | | |
| | | | | | | | | | | | | | | | | | | | | | | | | | 28 | | | | | |
| | | | | | | | | | | | | | | | | | | | | | | | | | 29 | | | | | |
| | | | | | | | | | | | | | | | | | | | | | | | | | 30 | | | | | |
| | | | | | | | | | | | | | | | | | | | | | | | | | 31 | | | | | |
| | | | | | | | | | | | | | | | | | | | | | | | | | 32 | | | | | |
| | | | | | | | | | | | | | | | | | | | | | | | | | 33 | | | | | |
| | | | | | | | | | | | | | | | | | | | | | | | | | 34 | | | | | |
| | | | | | | | | | | | | | | | | | | | | | | | | | 35 | | | | | |
| | | | | | | | | | | | | | | | | | | | | | | | | | 36 | | | | | |

# Subject_____

| Week | Week____ | | | | | Week____ | | | | | Week____ | | | | | Week____ | | | | | Week____ | | | | |
|---|---|---|---|---|---|---|---|---|---|---|---|---|---|---|---|---|---|---|---|---|---|---|---|---|---|
| Day | M | T | W | T | F | M | T | W | T | F | M | T | W | T | F | M | T | W | T | F | M | T | W | T | F |
| Date | | | | | | | | | | | | | | | | | | | | | | | | | |
| Assignments or Attendance | | | | | | | | | | | | | | | | | | | | | | | | | |
| **Name** | | | | | | | | | | | | | | | | | | | | | | | | | |
| 1 | | | | | | | | | | | | | | | | | | | | | | | | | |
| 2 | | | | | | | | | | | | | | | | | | | | | | | | | |
| 3 | | | | | | | | | | | | | | | | | | | | | | | | | |
| 4 | | | | | | | | | | | | | | | | | | | | | | | | | |
| 5 | | | | | | | | | | | | | | | | | | | | | | | | | |
| 6 | | | | | | | | | | | | | | | | | | | | | | | | | |
| 7 | | | | | | | | | | | | | | | | | | | | | | | | | |
| 8 | | | | | | | | | | | | | | | | | | | | | | | | | |
| 9 | | | | | | | | | | | | | | | | | | | | | | | | | |
| 10 | | | | | | | | | | | | | | | | | | | | | | | | | |
| 11 | | | | | | | | | | | | | | | | | | | | | | | | | |
| 12 | | | | | | | | | | | | | | | | | | | | | | | | | |
| 13 | | | | | | | | | | | | | | | | | | | | | | | | | |
| 14 | | | | | | | | | | | | | | | | | | | | | | | | | |
| 15 | | | | | | | | | | | | | | | | | | | | | | | | | |
| 16 | | | | | | | | | | | | | | | | | | | | | | | | | |
| 17 | | | | | | | | | | | | | | | | | | | | | | | | | |
| 18 | | | | | | | | | | | | | | | | | | | | | | | | | |
| 19 | | | | | | | | | | | | | | | | | | | | | | | | | |
| 20 | | | | | | | | | | | | | | | | | | | | | | | | | |
| 21 | | | | | | | | | | | | | | | | | | | | | | | | | |
| 22 | | | | | | | | | | | | | | | | | | | | | | | | | |
| 23 | | | | | | | | | | | | | | | | | | | | | | | | | |
| 24 | | | | | | | | | | | | | | | | | | | | | | | | | |
| 25 | | | | | | | | | | | | | | | | | | | | | | | | | |
| 26 | | | | | | | | | | | | | | | | | | | | | | | | | |
| 27 | | | | | | | | | | | | | | | | | | | | | | | | | |
| 28 | | | | | | | | | | | | | | | | | | | | | | | | | |
| 29 | | | | | | | | | | | | | | | | | | | | | | | | | |
| 30 | | | | | | | | | | | | | | | | | | | | | | | | | |
| 31 | | | | | | | | | | | | | | | | | | | | | | | | | |
| 32 | | | | | | | | | | | | | | | | | | | | | | | | | |
| 33 | | | | | | | | | | | | | | | | | | | | | | | | | |
| 34 | | | | | | | | | | | | | | | | | | | | | | | | | |
| 35 | | | | | | | | | | | | | | | | | | | | | | | | | |
| 36 | | | | | | | | | | | | | | | | | | | | | | | | | |

# Period

| Week____ | | | | | Week____ | | | | | Week____ | | | | | Week____ | | | | | Week____ | | | | | | Days Present | Days Absent | Tardies | Quarter Grade | | |
|---|---|---|---|---|---|---|---|---|---|---|---|---|---|---|---|---|---|---|---|---|---|---|---|---|---|---|---|---|---|---|---|
| M | T | W | T | F | M | T | W | T | F | M | T | W | T | F | M | T | W | T | F | M | T | W | T | F | | | | | | | |
| | | | | | | | | | | | | | | | | | | | | | | | | | 1 | | | | | | |
| | | | | | | | | | | | | | | | | | | | | | | | | | 2 | | | | | | |
| | | | | | | | | | | | | | | | | | | | | | | | | | 3 | | | | | | |
| | | | | | | | | | | | | | | | | | | | | | | | | | 4 | | | | | | |
| | | | | | | | | | | | | | | | | | | | | | | | | | 5 | | | | | | |
| | | | | | | | | | | | | | | | | | | | | | | | | | 6 | | | | | | |
| | | | | | | | | | | | | | | | | | | | | | | | | | 7 | | | | | | |
| | | | | | | | | | | | | | | | | | | | | | | | | | 8 | | | | | | |
| | | | | | | | | | | | | | | | | | | | | | | | | | 9 | | | | | | |
| | | | | | | | | | | | | | | | | | | | | | | | | | 10 | | | | | | |
| | | | | | | | | | | | | | | | | | | | | | | | | | 11 | | | | | | |
| | | | | | | | | | | | | | | | | | | | | | | | | | 12 | | | | | | |
| | | | | | | | | | | | | | | | | | | | | | | | | | 13 | | | | | | |
| | | | | | | | | | | | | | | | | | | | | | | | | | 14 | | | | | | |
| | | | | | | | | | | | | | | | | | | | | | | | | | 15 | | | | | | |
| | | | | | | | | | | | | | | | | | | | | | | | | | 16 | | | | | | |
| | | | | | | | | | | | | | | | | | | | | | | | | | 17 | | | | | | |
| | | | | | | | | | | | | | | | | | | | | | | | | | 18 | | | | | | |
| | | | | | | | | | | | | | | | | | | | | | | | | | 19 | | | | | | |
| | | | | | | | | | | | | | | | | | | | | | | | | | 20 | | | | | | |
| | | | | | | | | | | | | | | | | | | | | | | | | | 21 | | | | | | |
| | | | | | | | | | | | | | | | | | | | | | | | | | 22 | | | | | | |
| | | | | | | | | | | | | | | | | | | | | | | | | | 23 | | | | | | |
| | | | | | | | | | | | | | | | | | | | | | | | | | 24 | | | | | | |
| | | | | | | | | | | | | | | | | | | | | | | | | | 25 | | | | | | |
| | | | | | | | | | | | | | | | | | | | | | | | | | 26 | | | | | | |
| | | | | | | | | | | | | | | | | | | | | | | | | | 27 | | | | | | |
| | | | | | | | | | | | | | | | | | | | | | | | | | 28 | | | | | | |
| | | | | | | | | | | | | | | | | | | | | | | | | | 29 | | | | | | |
| | | | | | | | | | | | | | | | | | | | | | | | | | 30 | | | | | | |
| | | | | | | | | | | | | | | | | | | | | | | | | | 31 | | | | | | |
| | | | | | | | | | | | | | | | | | | | | | | | | | 32 | | | | | | |
| | | | | | | | | | | | | | | | | | | | | | | | | | 33 | | | | | | |
| | | | | | | | | | | | | | | | | | | | | | | | | | 34 | | | | | | |
| | | | | | | | | | | | | | | | | | | | | | | | | | 35 | | | | | | |
| | | | | | | | | | | | | | | | | | | | | | | | | | 36 | | | | | | |

# Subject_____

| Week | Week____ | | | | | Week____ | | | | | Week____ | | | | | Week____ | | | | | Week____ | | | | |
|---|---|---|---|---|---|---|---|---|---|---|---|---|---|---|---|---|---|---|---|---|---|---|---|---|---|
| Day | M | T | W | T | F | M | T | W | T | F | M | T | W | T | F | M | T | W | T | F | M | T | W | T | F |
| Date | | | | | | | | | | | | | | | | | | | | | | | | | |
| Assignments or Attendance | | | | | | | | | | | | | | | | | | | | | | | | | |
| Name | | | | | | | | | | | | | | | | | | | | | | | | | |
| 1 | | | | | | | | | | | | | | | | | | | | | | | | | |
| 2 | | | | | | | | | | | | | | | | | | | | | | | | | |
| 3 | | | | | | | | | | | | | | | | | | | | | | | | | |
| 4 | | | | | | | | | | | | | | | | | | | | | | | | | |
| 5 | | | | | | | | | | | | | | | | | | | | | | | | | |
| 6 | | | | | | | | | | | | | | | | | | | | | | | | | |
| 7 | | | | | | | | | | | | | | | | | | | | | | | | | |
| 8 | | | | | | | | | | | | | | | | | | | | | | | | | |
| 9 | | | | | | | | | | | | | | | | | | | | | | | | | |
| 10 | | | | | | | | | | | | | | | | | | | | | | | | | |
| 11 | | | | | | | | | | | | | | | | | | | | | | | | | |
| 12 | | | | | | | | | | | | | | | | | | | | | | | | | |
| 13 | | | | | | | | | | | | | | | | | | | | | | | | | |
| 14 | | | | | | | | | | | | | | | | | | | | | | | | | |
| 15 | | | | | | | | | | | | | | | | | | | | | | | | | |
| 16 | | | | | | | | | | | | | | | | | | | | | | | | | |
| 17 | | | | | | | | | | | | | | | | | | | | | | | | | |
| 18 | | | | | | | | | | | | | | | | | | | | | | | | | |
| 19 | | | | | | | | | | | | | | | | | | | | | | | | | |
| 20 | | | | | | | | | | | | | | | | | | | | | | | | | |
| 21 | | | | | | | | | | | | | | | | | | | | | | | | | |
| 22 | | | | | | | | | | | | | | | | | | | | | | | | | |
| 23 | | | | | | | | | | | | | | | | | | | | | | | | | |
| 24 | | | | | | | | | | | | | | | | | | | | | | | | | |
| 25 | | | | | | | | | | | | | | | | | | | | | | | | | |
| 26 | | | | | | | | | | | | | | | | | | | | | | | | | |
| 27 | | | | | | | | | | | | | | | | | | | | | | | | | |
| 28 | | | | | | | | | | | | | | | | | | | | | | | | | |
| 29 | | | | | | | | | | | | | | | | | | | | | | | | | |
| 30 | | | | | | | | | | | | | | | | | | | | | | | | | |
| 31 | | | | | | | | | | | | | | | | | | | | | | | | | |
| 32 | | | | | | | | | | | | | | | | | | | | | | | | | |
| 33 | | | | | | | | | | | | | | | | | | | | | | | | | |
| 34 | | | | | | | | | | | | | | | | | | | | | | | | | |
| 35 | | | | | | | | | | | | | | | | | | | | | | | | | |
| 36 | | | | | | | | | | | | | | | | | | | | | | | | | |

# Period_____

| Week____ | | | | Week____ | | | | Week____ | | | | Week____ | | | | Week____ | | | | | Days Present | Days Absent | Tardies | Quarter Grade | | |
|---|---|---|---|---|---|---|---|---|---|---|---|---|---|---|---|---|---|---|---|---|---|---|---|---|---|---|
| M | T | W | T | F | M | T | W | T | F | M | T | W | T | F | M | T | W | T | F | M | T | W | T | F | | | | | | |
| | | | | | | | | | | | | | | | | | | | | | | | | | | | | | | |
| | | | | | | | | | | | | | | | | | | | | | | | | | | | | | | |
| | | | | | | | | | | | | | | | | | | | | | | | | | 1 | | | | | |
| | | | | | | | | | | | | | | | | | | | | | | | | | 2 | | | | | |
| | | | | | | | | | | | | | | | | | | | | | | | | | 3 | | | | | |
| | | | | | | | | | | | | | | | | | | | | | | | | | 4 | | | | | |
| | | | | | | | | | | | | | | | | | | | | | | | | | 5 | | | | | |
| | | | | | | | | | | | | | | | | | | | | | | | | | 6 | | | | | |
| | | | | | | | | | | | | | | | | | | | | | | | | | 7 | | | | | |
| | | | | | | | | | | | | | | | | | | | | | | | | | 8 | | | | | |
| | | | | | | | | | | | | | | | | | | | | | | | | | 9 | | | | | |
| | | | | | | | | | | | | | | | | | | | | | | | | | 10 | | | | | |
| | | | | | | | | | | | | | | | | | | | | | | | | | 11 | | | | | |
| | | | | | | | | | | | | | | | | | | | | | | | | | 12 | | | | | |
| | | | | | | | | | | | | | | | | | | | | | | | | | 13 | | | | | |
| | | | | | | | | | | | | | | | | | | | | | | | | | 14 | | | | | |
| | | | | | | | | | | | | | | | | | | | | | | | | | 15 | | | | | |
| | | | | | | | | | | | | | | | | | | | | | | | | | 16 | | | | | |
| | | | | | | | | | | | | | | | | | | | | | | | | | 17 | | | | | |
| | | | | | | | | | | | | | | | | | | | | | | | | | 18 | | | | | |
| | | | | | | | | | | | | | | | | | | | | | | | | | 19 | | | | | |
| | | | | | | | | | | | | | | | | | | | | | | | | | 20 | | | | | |
| | | | | | | | | | | | | | | | | | | | | | | | | | 21 | | | | | |
| | | | | | | | | | | | | | | | | | | | | | | | | | 22 | | | | | |
| | | | | | | | | | | | | | | | | | | | | | | | | | 23 | | | | | |
| | | | | | | | | | | | | | | | | | | | | | | | | | 24 | | | | | |
| | | | | | | | | | | | | | | | | | | | | | | | | | 25 | | | | | |
| | | | | | | | | | | | | | | | | | | | | | | | | | 26 | | | | | |
| | | | | | | | | | | | | | | | | | | | | | | | | | 27 | | | | | |
| | | | | | | | | | | | | | | | | | | | | | | | | | 28 | | | | | |
| | | | | | | | | | | | | | | | | | | | | | | | | | 29 | | | | | |
| | | | | | | | | | | | | | | | | | | | | | | | | | 30 | | | | | |
| | | | | | | | | | | | | | | | | | | | | | | | | | 31 | | | | | |
| | | | | | | | | | | | | | | | | | | | | | | | | | 32 | | | | | |
| | | | | | | | | | | | | | | | | | | | | | | | | | 33 | | | | | |
| | | | | | | | | | | | | | | | | | | | | | | | | | 34 | | | | | |
| | | | | | | | | | | | | | | | | | | | | | | | | | 35 | | | | | |
| | | | | | | | | | | | | | | | | | | | | | | | | | 36 | | | | | |

# Subject_____

| Week | Week____ | | | | | Week____ | | | | | Week____ | | | | | Week____ | | | | | Week____ | | | | |
|---|---|---|---|---|---|---|---|---|---|---|---|---|---|---|---|---|---|---|---|---|---|---|---|---|---|
| Day | M | T | W | T | F | M | T | W | T | F | M | T | W | T | F | M | T | W | T | F | M | T | W | T | F |
| Date | | | | | | | | | | | | | | | | | | | | | | | | | |
| Assignments or Attendance | | | | | | | | | | | | | | | | | | | | | | | | | |
| Name | | | | | | | | | | | | | | | | | | | | | | | | | |
| 1 | | | | | | | | | | | | | | | | | | | | | | | | | |
| 2 | | | | | | | | | | | | | | | | | | | | | | | | | |
| 3 | | | | | | | | | | | | | | | | | | | | | | | | | |
| 4 | | | | | | | | | | | | | | | | | | | | | | | | | |
| 5 | | | | | | | | | | | | | | | | | | | | | | | | | |
| 6 | | | | | | | | | | | | | | | | | | | | | | | | | |
| 7 | | | | | | | | | | | | | | | | | | | | | | | | | |
| 8 | | | | | | | | | | | | | | | | | | | | | | | | | |
| 9 | | | | | | | | | | | | | | | | | | | | | | | | | |
| 10 | | | | | | | | | | | | | | | | | | | | | | | | | |
| 11 | | | | | | | | | | | | | | | | | | | | | | | | | |
| 12 | | | | | | | | | | | | | | | | | | | | | | | | | |
| 13 | | | | | | | | | | | | | | | | | | | | | | | | | |
| 14 | | | | | | | | | | | | | | | | | | | | | | | | | |
| 15 | | | | | | | | | | | | | | | | | | | | | | | | | |
| 16 | | | | | | | | | | | | | | | | | | | | | | | | | |
| 17 | | | | | | | | | | | | | | | | | | | | | | | | | |
| 18 | | | | | | | | | | | | | | | | | | | | | | | | | |
| 19 | | | | | | | | | | | | | | | | | | | | | | | | | |
| 20 | | | | | | | | | | | | | | | | | | | | | | | | | |
| 21 | | | | | | | | | | | | | | | | | | | | | | | | | |
| 22 | | | | | | | | | | | | | | | | | | | | | | | | | |
| 23 | | | | | | | | | | | | | | | | | | | | | | | | | |
| 24 | | | | | | | | | | | | | | | | | | | | | | | | | |
| 25 | | | | | | | | | | | | | | | | | | | | | | | | | |
| 26 | | | | | | | | | | | | | | | | | | | | | | | | | |
| 27 | | | | | | | | | | | | | | | | | | | | | | | | | |
| 28 | | | | | | | | | | | | | | | | | | | | | | | | | |
| 29 | | | | | | | | | | | | | | | | | | | | | | | | | |
| 30 | | | | | | | | | | | | | | | | | | | | | | | | | |
| 31 | | | | | | | | | | | | | | | | | | | | | | | | | |
| 32 | | | | | | | | | | | | | | | | | | | | | | | | | |
| 33 | | | | | | | | | | | | | | | | | | | | | | | | | |
| 34 | | | | | | | | | | | | | | | | | | | | | | | | | |
| 35 | | | | | | | | | | | | | | | | | | | | | | | | | |
| 36 | | | | | | | | | | | | | | | | | | | | | | | | | |

# Period_____

| Week____ | | | | | Week____ | | | | | Week____ | | | | | Week____ | | | | | Week____ | | | | | | Days Present | Days Absent | Tardies | Quarter Grade | |
|---|---|---|---|---|---|---|---|---|---|---|---|---|---|---|---|---|---|---|---|---|---|---|---|---|---|---|---|---|---|---|
| M | T | W | T | F | M | T | W | T | F | M | T | W | T | F | M | T | W | T | F | M | T | W | T | F | | | | | | |
| | | | | | | | | | | | | | | | | | | | | | | | | | 1 | | | | | |
| | | | | | | | | | | | | | | | | | | | | | | | | | 2 | | | | | |
| | | | | | | | | | | | | | | | | | | | | | | | | | 3 | | | | | |
| | | | | | | | | | | | | | | | | | | | | | | | | | 4 | | | | | |
| | | | | | | | | | | | | | | | | | | | | | | | | | 5 | | | | | |
| | | | | | | | | | | | | | | | | | | | | | | | | | 6 | | | | | |
| | | | | | | | | | | | | | | | | | | | | | | | | | 7 | | | | | |
| | | | | | | | | | | | | | | | | | | | | | | | | | 8 | | | | | |
| | | | | | | | | | | | | | | | | | | | | | | | | | 9 | | | | | |
| | | | | | | | | | | | | | | | | | | | | | | | | | 10 | | | | | |
| | | | | | | | | | | | | | | | | | | | | | | | | | 11 | | | | | |
| | | | | | | | | | | | | | | | | | | | | | | | | | 12 | | | | | |
| | | | | | | | | | | | | | | | | | | | | | | | | | 13 | | | | | |
| | | | | | | | | | | | | | | | | | | | | | | | | | 14 | | | | | |
| | | | | | | | | | | | | | | | | | | | | | | | | | 15 | | | | | |
| | | | | | | | | | | | | | | | | | | | | | | | | | 16 | | | | | |
| | | | | | | | | | | | | | | | | | | | | | | | | | 17 | | | | | |
| | | | | | | | | | | | | | | | | | | | | | | | | | 18 | | | | | |
| | | | | | | | | | | | | | | | | | | | | | | | | | 19 | | | | | |
| | | | | | | | | | | | | | | | | | | | | | | | | | 20 | | | | | |
| | | | | | | | | | | | | | | | | | | | | | | | | | 21 | | | | | |
| | | | | | | | | | | | | | | | | | | | | | | | | | 22 | | | | | |
| | | | | | | | | | | | | | | | | | | | | | | | | | 23 | | | | | |
| | | | | | | | | | | | | | | | | | | | | | | | | | 24 | | | | | |
| | | | | | | | | | | | | | | | | | | | | | | | | | 25 | | | | | |
| | | | | | | | | | | | | | | | | | | | | | | | | | 26 | | | | | |
| | | | | | | | | | | | | | | | | | | | | | | | | | 27 | | | | | |
| | | | | | | | | | | | | | | | | | | | | | | | | | 28 | | | | | |
| | | | | | | | | | | | | | | | | | | | | | | | | | 29 | | | | | |
| | | | | | | | | | | | | | | | | | | | | | | | | | 30 | | | | | |
| | | | | | | | | | | | | | | | | | | | | | | | | | 31 | | | | | |
| | | | | | | | | | | | | | | | | | | | | | | | | | 32 | | | | | |
| | | | | | | | | | | | | | | | | | | | | | | | | | 33 | | | | | |
| | | | | | | | | | | | | | | | | | | | | | | | | | 34 | | | | | |
| | | | | | | | | | | | | | | | | | | | | | | | | | 35 | | | | | |
| | | | | | | | | | | | | | | | | | | | | | | | | | 36 | | | | | |

# Subject_____

| Week | Week\_\_\_\_ | | | | | Week\_\_\_\_ | | | | | Week\_\_\_\_ | | | | | Week\_\_\_\_ | | | | | Week\_\_\_\_ | | | | |
|---|---|---|---|---|---|---|---|---|---|---|---|---|---|---|---|---|---|---|---|---|---|---|---|---|---|
| Day | M | T | W | T | F | M | T | W | T | F | M | T | W | T | F | M | T | W | T | F | M | T | W | T | F |
| Date | | | | | | | | | | | | | | | | | | | | | | | | | |
| Assignments or Attendance | | | | | | | | | | | | | | | | | | | | | | | | | |
| Name | | | | | | | | | | | | | | | | | | | | | | | | | |
| 1 | | | | | | | | | | | | | | | | | | | | | | | | | |
| 2 | | | | | | | | | | | | | | | | | | | | | | | | | |
| 3 | | | | | | | | | | | | | | | | | | | | | | | | | |
| 4 | | | | | | | | | | | | | | | | | | | | | | | | | |
| 5 | | | | | | | | | | | | | | | | | | | | | | | | | |
| 6 | | | | | | | | | | | | | | | | | | | | | | | | | |
| 7 | | | | | | | | | | | | | | | | | | | | | | | | | |
| 8 | | | | | | | | | | | | | | | | | | | | | | | | | |
| 9 | | | | | | | | | | | | | | | | | | | | | | | | | |
| 10 | | | | | | | | | | | | | | | | | | | | | | | | | |
| 11 | | | | | | | | | | | | | | | | | | | | | | | | | |
| 12 | | | | | | | | | | | | | | | | | | | | | | | | | |
| 13 | | | | | | | | | | | | | | | | | | | | | | | | | |
| 14 | | | | | | | | | | | | | | | | | | | | | | | | | |
| 15 | | | | | | | | | | | | | | | | | | | | | | | | | |
| 16 | | | | | | | | | | | | | | | | | | | | | | | | | |
| 17 | | | | | | | | | | | | | | | | | | | | | | | | | |
| 18 | | | | | | | | | | | | | | | | | | | | | | | | | |
| 19 | | | | | | | | | | | | | | | | | | | | | | | | | |
| 20 | | | | | | | | | | | | | | | | | | | | | | | | | |
| 21 | | | | | | | | | | | | | | | | | | | | | | | | | |
| 22 | | | | | | | | | | | | | | | | | | | | | | | | | |
| 23 | | | | | | | | | | | | | | | | | | | | | | | | | |
| 24 | | | | | | | | | | | | | | | | | | | | | | | | | |
| 25 | | | | | | | | | | | | | | | | | | | | | | | | | |
| 26 | | | | | | | | | | | | | | | | | | | | | | | | | |
| 27 | | | | | | | | | | | | | | | | | | | | | | | | | |
| 28 | | | | | | | | | | | | | | | | | | | | | | | | | |
| 29 | | | | | | | | | | | | | | | | | | | | | | | | | |
| 30 | | | | | | | | | | | | | | | | | | | | | | | | | |
| 31 | | | | | | | | | | | | | | | | | | | | | | | | | |
| 32 | | | | | | | | | | | | | | | | | | | | | | | | | |
| 33 | | | | | | | | | | | | | | | | | | | | | | | | | |
| 34 | | | | | | | | | | | | | | | | | | | | | | | | | |
| 35 | | | | | | | | | | | | | | | | | | | | | | | | | |
| 36 | | | | | | | | | | | | | | | | | | | | | | | | | |

# Period_____

| Week____ | | | | | Week____ | | | | | Week____ | | | | | Week____ | | | | | Week____ | | | | | | Days Present | Days Absent | Tardies | Quarter Grade | | |
|---|---|---|---|---|---|---|---|---|---|---|---|---|---|---|---|---|---|---|---|---|---|---|---|---|---|---|---|---|---|---|---|
| M | T | W | T | F | M | T | W | T | F | M | T | W | T | F | M | T | W | T | F | M | T | W | T | F | | | | | | | |
| | | | | | | | | | | | | | | | | | | | | | | | | | 1 | | | | | | |
| | | | | | | | | | | | | | | | | | | | | | | | | | 2 | | | | | | |
| | | | | | | | | | | | | | | | | | | | | | | | | | 3 | | | | | | |
| | | | | | | | | | | | | | | | | | | | | | | | | | 4 | | | | | | |
| | | | | | | | | | | | | | | | | | | | | | | | | | 5 | | | | | | |
| | | | | | | | | | | | | | | | | | | | | | | | | | 6 | | | | | | |
| | | | | | | | | | | | | | | | | | | | | | | | | | 7 | | | | | | |
| | | | | | | | | | | | | | | | | | | | | | | | | | 8 | | | | | | |
| | | | | | | | | | | | | | | | | | | | | | | | | | 9 | | | | | | |
| | | | | | | | | | | | | | | | | | | | | | | | | | 10 | | | | | | |
| | | | | | | | | | | | | | | | | | | | | | | | | | 11 | | | | | | |
| | | | | | | | | | | | | | | | | | | | | | | | | | 12 | | | | | | |
| | | | | | | | | | | | | | | | | | | | | | | | | | 13 | | | | | | |
| | | | | | | | | | | | | | | | | | | | | | | | | | 14 | | | | | | |
| | | | | | | | | | | | | | | | | | | | | | | | | | 15 | | | | | | |
| | | | | | | | | | | | | | | | | | | | | | | | | | 16 | | | | | | |
| | | | | | | | | | | | | | | | | | | | | | | | | | 17 | | | | | | |
| | | | | | | | | | | | | | | | | | | | | | | | | | 18 | | | | | | |
| | | | | | | | | | | | | | | | | | | | | | | | | | 19 | | | | | | |
| | | | | | | | | | | | | | | | | | | | | | | | | | 20 | | | | | | |
| | | | | | | | | | | | | | | | | | | | | | | | | | 21 | | | | | | |
| | | | | | | | | | | | | | | | | | | | | | | | | | 22 | | | | | | |
| | | | | | | | | | | | | | | | | | | | | | | | | | 23 | | | | | | |
| | | | | | | | | | | | | | | | | | | | | | | | | | 24 | | | | | | |
| | | | | | | | | | | | | | | | | | | | | | | | | | 25 | | | | | | |
| | | | | | | | | | | | | | | | | | | | | | | | | | 26 | | | | | | |
| | | | | | | | | | | | | | | | | | | | | | | | | | 27 | | | | | | |
| | | | | | | | | | | | | | | | | | | | | | | | | | 28 | | | | | | |
| | | | | | | | | | | | | | | | | | | | | | | | | | 29 | | | | | | |
| | | | | | | | | | | | | | | | | | | | | | | | | | 30 | | | | | | |
| | | | | | | | | | | | | | | | | | | | | | | | | | 31 | | | | | | |
| | | | | | | | | | | | | | | | | | | | | | | | | | 32 | | | | | | |
| | | | | | | | | | | | | | | | | | | | | | | | | | 33 | | | | | | |
| | | | | | | | | | | | | | | | | | | | | | | | | | 34 | | | | | | |
| | | | | | | | | | | | | | | | | | | | | | | | | | 35 | | | | | | |
| | | | | | | | | | | | | | | | | | | | | | | | | | 36 | | | | | | |

# Subject＿＿＿＿＿＿＿＿＿＿＿＿＿＿＿＿

| Week | Week＿＿ | | | | | Week＿＿ | | | | | Week＿＿ | | | | | Week＿＿ | | | | | Week＿＿ | | | | |
|---|---|---|---|---|---|---|---|---|---|---|---|---|---|---|---|---|---|---|---|---|---|---|---|---|---|
| Day | M | T | W | T | F | M | T | W | T | F | M | T | W | T | F | M | T | W | T | F | M | T | W | T | F |
| Date | | | | | | | | | | | | | | | | | | | | | | | | | |
| Assignments or Attendance | | | | | | | | | | | | | | | | | | | | | | | | | |
| Name | | | | | | | | | | | | | | | | | | | | | | | | | |
| 1 | | | | | | | | | | | | | | | | | | | | | | | | | |
| 2 | | | | | | | | | | | | | | | | | | | | | | | | | |
| 3 | | | | | | | | | | | | | | | | | | | | | | | | | |
| 4 | | | | | | | | | | | | | | | | | | | | | | | | | |
| 5 | | | | | | | | | | | | | | | | | | | | | | | | | |
| 6 | | | | | | | | | | | | | | | | | | | | | | | | | |
| 7 | | | | | | | | | | | | | | | | | | | | | | | | | |
| 8 | | | | | | | | | | | | | | | | | | | | | | | | | |
| 9 | | | | | | | | | | | | | | | | | | | | | | | | | |
| 10 | | | | | | | | | | | | | | | | | | | | | | | | | |
| 11 | | | | | | | | | | | | | | | | | | | | | | | | | |
| 12 | | | | | | | | | | | | | | | | | | | | | | | | | |
| 13 | | | | | | | | | | | | | | | | | | | | | | | | | |
| 14 | | | | | | | | | | | | | | | | | | | | | | | | | |
| 15 | | | | | | | | | | | | | | | | | | | | | | | | | |
| 16 | | | | | | | | | | | | | | | | | | | | | | | | | |
| 17 | | | | | | | | | | | | | | | | | | | | | | | | | |
| 18 | | | | | | | | | | | | | | | | | | | | | | | | | |
| 19 | | | | | | | | | | | | | | | | | | | | | | | | | |
| 20 | | | | | | | | | | | | | | | | | | | | | | | | | |
| 21 | | | | | | | | | | | | | | | | | | | | | | | | | |
| 22 | | | | | | | | | | | | | | | | | | | | | | | | | |
| 23 | | | | | | | | | | | | | | | | | | | | | | | | | |
| 24 | | | | | | | | | | | | | | | | | | | | | | | | | |
| 25 | | | | | | | | | | | | | | | | | | | | | | | | | |
| 26 | | | | | | | | | | | | | | | | | | | | | | | | | |
| 27 | | | | | | | | | | | | | | | | | | | | | | | | | |
| 28 | | | | | | | | | | | | | | | | | | | | | | | | | |
| 29 | | | | | | | | | | | | | | | | | | | | | | | | | |
| 30 | | | | | | | | | | | | | | | | | | | | | | | | | |
| 31 | | | | | | | | | | | | | | | | | | | | | | | | | |
| 32 | | | | | | | | | | | | | | | | | | | | | | | | | |
| 33 | | | | | | | | | | | | | | | | | | | | | | | | | |
| 34 | | | | | | | | | | | | | | | | | | | | | | | | | |
| 35 | | | | | | | | | | | | | | | | | | | | | | | | | |
| 36 | | | | | | | | | | | | | | | | | | | | | | | | | |

# Period

| Week____ | | | | | Week____ | | | | | Week____ | | | | | Week____ | | | | | Week____ | | | | | | Days Present | Days Absent | Tardies | Quarter Grade | | |
|---|---|---|---|---|---|---|---|---|---|---|---|---|---|---|---|---|---|---|---|---|---|---|---|---|---|---|---|---|---|---|
| M | T | W | T | F | M | T | W | T | F | M | T | W | T | F | M | T | W | T | F | M | T | W | T | F | | | | | | |
| | | | | | | | | | | | | | | | | | | | | | | | | | 1 | | | | | |
| | | | | | | | | | | | | | | | | | | | | | | | | | 2 | | | | | |
| | | | | | | | | | | | | | | | | | | | | | | | | | 3 | | | | | |
| | | | | | | | | | | | | | | | | | | | | | | | | | 4 | | | | | |
| | | | | | | | | | | | | | | | | | | | | | | | | | 5 | | | | | |
| | | | | | | | | | | | | | | | | | | | | | | | | | 6 | | | | | |
| | | | | | | | | | | | | | | | | | | | | | | | | | 7 | | | | | |
| | | | | | | | | | | | | | | | | | | | | | | | | | 8 | | | | | |
| | | | | | | | | | | | | | | | | | | | | | | | | | 9 | | | | | |
| | | | | | | | | | | | | | | | | | | | | | | | | | 10 | | | | | |
| | | | | | | | | | | | | | | | | | | | | | | | | | 11 | | | | | |
| | | | | | | | | | | | | | | | | | | | | | | | | | 12 | | | | | |
| | | | | | | | | | | | | | | | | | | | | | | | | | 13 | | | | | |
| | | | | | | | | | | | | | | | | | | | | | | | | | 14 | | | | | |
| | | | | | | | | | | | | | | | | | | | | | | | | | 15 | | | | | |
| | | | | | | | | | | | | | | | | | | | | | | | | | 16 | | | | | |
| | | | | | | | | | | | | | | | | | | | | | | | | | 17 | | | | | |
| | | | | | | | | | | | | | | | | | | | | | | | | | 18 | | | | | |
| | | | | | | | | | | | | | | | | | | | | | | | | | 19 | | | | | |
| | | | | | | | | | | | | | | | | | | | | | | | | | 20 | | | | | |
| | | | | | | | | | | | | | | | | | | | | | | | | | 21 | | | | | |
| | | | | | | | | | | | | | | | | | | | | | | | | | 22 | | | | | |
| | | | | | | | | | | | | | | | | | | | | | | | | | 23 | | | | | |
| | | | | | | | | | | | | | | | | | | | | | | | | | 24 | | | | | |
| | | | | | | | | | | | | | | | | | | | | | | | | | 25 | | | | | |
| | | | | | | | | | | | | | | | | | | | | | | | | | 26 | | | | | |
| | | | | | | | | | | | | | | | | | | | | | | | | | 27 | | | | | |
| | | | | | | | | | | | | | | | | | | | | | | | | | 28 | | | | | |
| | | | | | | | | | | | | | | | | | | | | | | | | | 29 | | | | | |
| | | | | | | | | | | | | | | | | | | | | | | | | | 30 | | | | | |
| | | | | | | | | | | | | | | | | | | | | | | | | | 31 | | | | | |
| | | | | | | | | | | | | | | | | | | | | | | | | | 32 | | | | | |
| | | | | | | | | | | | | | | | | | | | | | | | | | 33 | | | | | |
| | | | | | | | | | | | | | | | | | | | | | | | | | 34 | | | | | |
| | | | | | | | | | | | | | | | | | | | | | | | | | 35 | | | | | |
| | | | | | | | | | | | | | | | | | | | | | | | | | 36 | | | | | |

# Subject_____

| Week | Week____ | | | | | Week____ | | | | | Week____ | | | | | Week____ | | | | | Week____ | | | | |
|---|---|---|---|---|---|---|---|---|---|---|---|---|---|---|---|---|---|---|---|---|---|---|---|---|---|
| Day | M | T | W | T | F | M | T | W | T | F | M | T | W | T | F | M | T | W | T | F | M | T | W | T | F |
| Date | | | | | | | | | | | | | | | | | | | | | | | | | |
| Assignments or Attendance | | | | | | | | | | | | | | | | | | | | | | | | | |
| Name | | | | | | | | | | | | | | | | | | | | | | | | | |
| 1 | | | | | | | | | | | | | | | | | | | | | | | | | |
| 2 | | | | | | | | | | | | | | | | | | | | | | | | | |
| 3 | | | | | | | | | | | | | | | | | | | | | | | | | |
| 4 | | | | | | | | | | | | | | | | | | | | | | | | | |
| 5 | | | | | | | | | | | | | | | | | | | | | | | | | |
| 6 | | | | | | | | | | | | | | | | | | | | | | | | | |
| 7 | | | | | | | | | | | | | | | | | | | | | | | | | |
| 8 | | | | | | | | | | | | | | | | | | | | | | | | | |
| 9 | | | | | | | | | | | | | | | | | | | | | | | | | |
| 10 | | | | | | | | | | | | | | | | | | | | | | | | | |
| 11 | | | | | | | | | | | | | | | | | | | | | | | | | |
| 12 | | | | | | | | | | | | | | | | | | | | | | | | | |
| 13 | | | | | | | | | | | | | | | | | | | | | | | | | |
| 14 | | | | | | | | | | | | | | | | | | | | | | | | | |
| 15 | | | | | | | | | | | | | | | | | | | | | | | | | |
| 16 | | | | | | | | | | | | | | | | | | | | | | | | | |
| 17 | | | | | | | | | | | | | | | | | | | | | | | | | |
| 18 | | | | | | | | | | | | | | | | | | | | | | | | | |
| 19 | | | | | | | | | | | | | | | | | | | | | | | | | |
| 20 | | | | | | | | | | | | | | | | | | | | | | | | | |
| 21 | | | | | | | | | | | | | | | | | | | | | | | | | |
| 22 | | | | | | | | | | | | | | | | | | | | | | | | | |
| 23 | | | | | | | | | | | | | | | | | | | | | | | | | |
| 24 | | | | | | | | | | | | | | | | | | | | | | | | | |
| 25 | | | | | | | | | | | | | | | | | | | | | | | | | |
| 26 | | | | | | | | | | | | | | | | | | | | | | | | | |
| 27 | | | | | | | | | | | | | | | | | | | | | | | | | |
| 28 | | | | | | | | | | | | | | | | | | | | | | | | | |
| 29 | | | | | | | | | | | | | | | | | | | | | | | | | |
| 30 | | | | | | | | | | | | | | | | | | | | | | | | | |
| 31 | | | | | | | | | | | | | | | | | | | | | | | | | |
| 32 | | | | | | | | | | | | | | | | | | | | | | | | | |
| 33 | | | | | | | | | | | | | | | | | | | | | | | | | |
| 34 | | | | | | | | | | | | | | | | | | | | | | | | | |
| 35 | | | | | | | | | | | | | | | | | | | | | | | | | |
| 36 | | | | | | | | | | | | | | | | | | | | | | | | | |

# Period_____

| Week____ | | | | | Week____ | | | | | Week____ | | | | | Week____ | | | | | Week____ | | | | | | Days Present | Days Absent | Tardies | Quarter Grade | |
|---|---|---|---|---|---|---|---|---|---|---|---|---|---|---|---|---|---|---|---|---|---|---|---|---|---|---|---|---|---|---|
| M | T | W | T | F | M | T | W | T | F | M | T | W | T | F | M | T | W | T | F | M | T | W | T | F | | | | | | |
| | | | | | | | | | | | | | | | | | | | | | | | | | | | | | | |
| | | | | | | | | | | | | | | | | | | | | | | | | | | | | | | |
| | | | | | | | | | | | | | | | | | | | | | | | | | 1 | | | | | |
| | | | | | | | | | | | | | | | | | | | | | | | | | 2 | | | | | |
| | | | | | | | | | | | | | | | | | | | | | | | | | 3 | | | | | |
| | | | | | | | | | | | | | | | | | | | | | | | | | 4 | | | | | |
| | | | | | | | | | | | | | | | | | | | | | | | | | 5 | | | | | |
| | | | | | | | | | | | | | | | | | | | | | | | | | 6 | | | | | |
| | | | | | | | | | | | | | | | | | | | | | | | | | 7 | | | | | |
| | | | | | | | | | | | | | | | | | | | | | | | | | 8 | | | | | |
| | | | | | | | | | | | | | | | | | | | | | | | | | 9 | | | | | |
| | | | | | | | | | | | | | | | | | | | | | | | | | 10 | | | | | |
| | | | | | | | | | | | | | | | | | | | | | | | | | 11 | | | | | |
| | | | | | | | | | | | | | | | | | | | | | | | | | 12 | | | | | |
| | | | | | | | | | | | | | | | | | | | | | | | | | 13 | | | | | |
| | | | | | | | | | | | | | | | | | | | | | | | | | 14 | | | | | |
| | | | | | | | | | | | | | | | | | | | | | | | | | 15 | | | | | |
| | | | | | | | | | | | | | | | | | | | | | | | | | 16 | | | | | |
| | | | | | | | | | | | | | | | | | | | | | | | | | 17 | | | | | |
| | | | | | | | | | | | | | | | | | | | | | | | | | 18 | | | | | |
| | | | | | | | | | | | | | | | | | | | | | | | | | 19 | | | | | |
| | | | | | | | | | | | | | | | | | | | | | | | | | 20 | | | | | |
| | | | | | | | | | | | | | | | | | | | | | | | | | 21 | | | | | |
| | | | | | | | | | | | | | | | | | | | | | | | | | 22 | | | | | |
| | | | | | | | | | | | | | | | | | | | | | | | | | 23 | | | | | |
| | | | | | | | | | | | | | | | | | | | | | | | | | 24 | | | | | |
| | | | | | | | | | | | | | | | | | | | | | | | | | 25 | | | | | |
| | | | | | | | | | | | | | | | | | | | | | | | | | 26 | | | | | |
| | | | | | | | | | | | | | | | | | | | | | | | | | 27 | | | | | |
| | | | | | | | | | | | | | | | | | | | | | | | | | 28 | | | | | |
| | | | | | | | | | | | | | | | | | | | | | | | | | 29 | | | | | |
| | | | | | | | | | | | | | | | | | | | | | | | | | 30 | | | | | |
| | | | | | | | | | | | | | | | | | | | | | | | | | 31 | | | | | |
| | | | | | | | | | | | | | | | | | | | | | | | | | 32 | | | | | |
| | | | | | | | | | | | | | | | | | | | | | | | | | 33 | | | | | |
| | | | | | | | | | | | | | | | | | | | | | | | | | 34 | | | | | |
| | | | | | | | | | | | | | | | | | | | | | | | | | 35 | | | | | |
| | | | | | | | | | | | | | | | | | | | | | | | | | 36 | | | | | |

# Subject _____

| Week | Week____ | | | | | Week____ | | | | | Week____ | | | | | Week____ | | | | | Week____ | | | | |
|---|---|---|---|---|---|---|---|---|---|---|---|---|---|---|---|---|---|---|---|---|---|---|---|---|---|
| Day | M | T | W | T | F | M | T | W | T | F | M | T | W | T | F | M | T | W | T | F | M | T | W | T | F |
| Date | | | | | | | | | | | | | | | | | | | | | | | | | |
| Assignments or Attendance | | | | | | | | | | | | | | | | | | | | | | | | | |
| Name | | | | | | | | | | | | | | | | | | | | | | | | | |
| 1 | | | | | | | | | | | | | | | | | | | | | | | | | |
| 2 | | | | | | | | | | | | | | | | | | | | | | | | | |
| 3 | | | | | | | | | | | | | | | | | | | | | | | | | |
| 4 | | | | | | | | | | | | | | | | | | | | | | | | | |
| 5 | | | | | | | | | | | | | | | | | | | | | | | | | |
| 6 | | | | | | | | | | | | | | | | | | | | | | | | | |
| 7 | | | | | | | | | | | | | | | | | | | | | | | | | |
| 8 | | | | | | | | | | | | | | | | | | | | | | | | | |
| 9 | | | | | | | | | | | | | | | | | | | | | | | | | |
| 10 | | | | | | | | | | | | | | | | | | | | | | | | | |
| 11 | | | | | | | | | | | | | | | | | | | | | | | | | |
| 12 | | | | | | | | | | | | | | | | | | | | | | | | | |
| 13 | | | | | | | | | | | | | | | | | | | | | | | | | |
| 14 | | | | | | | | | | | | | | | | | | | | | | | | | |
| 15 | | | | | | | | | | | | | | | | | | | | | | | | | |
| 16 | | | | | | | | | | | | | | | | | | | | | | | | | |
| 17 | | | | | | | | | | | | | | | | | | | | | | | | | |
| 18 | | | | | | | | | | | | | | | | | | | | | | | | | |
| 19 | | | | | | | | | | | | | | | | | | | | | | | | | |
| 20 | | | | | | | | | | | | | | | | | | | | | | | | | |
| 21 | | | | | | | | | | | | | | | | | | | | | | | | | |
| 22 | | | | | | | | | | | | | | | | | | | | | | | | | |
| 23 | | | | | | | | | | | | | | | | | | | | | | | | | |
| 24 | | | | | | | | | | | | | | | | | | | | | | | | | |
| 25 | | | | | | | | | | | | | | | | | | | | | | | | | |
| 26 | | | | | | | | | | | | | | | | | | | | | | | | | |
| 27 | | | | | | | | | | | | | | | | | | | | | | | | | |
| 28 | | | | | | | | | | | | | | | | | | | | | | | | | |
| 29 | | | | | | | | | | | | | | | | | | | | | | | | | |
| 30 | | | | | | | | | | | | | | | | | | | | | | | | | |
| 31 | | | | | | | | | | | | | | | | | | | | | | | | | |
| 32 | | | | | | | | | | | | | | | | | | | | | | | | | |
| 33 | | | | | | | | | | | | | | | | | | | | | | | | | |
| 34 | | | | | | | | | | | | | | | | | | | | | | | | | |
| 35 | | | | | | | | | | | | | | | | | | | | | | | | | |
| 36 | | | | | | | | | | | | | | | | | | | | | | | | | |

# Period

| Week____ | | | | | Week____ | | | | | Week____ | | | | | Week____ | | | | | Week____ | | | | | | Days Present | Days Absent | Tardies | Quarter Grade | |
|---|---|---|---|---|---|---|---|---|---|---|---|---|---|---|---|---|---|---|---|---|---|---|---|---|---|---|---|---|---|---|
| M | T | W | T | F | M | T | W | T | F | M | T | W | T | F | M | T | W | T | F | M | T | W | T | F | | | | | | |
| | | | | | | | | | | | | | | | | | | | | | | | | | | | | | | |
| | | | | | | | | | | | | | | | | | | | | | | | | | | | | | | |
| | | | | | | | | | | | | | | | | | | | | | | | | | 1 | | | | | |
| | | | | | | | | | | | | | | | | | | | | | | | | | 2 | | | | | |
| | | | | | | | | | | | | | | | | | | | | | | | | | 3 | | | | | |
| | | | | | | | | | | | | | | | | | | | | | | | | | 4 | | | | | |
| | | | | | | | | | | | | | | | | | | | | | | | | | 5 | | | | | |
| | | | | | | | | | | | | | | | | | | | | | | | | | 6 | | | | | |
| | | | | | | | | | | | | | | | | | | | | | | | | | 7 | | | | | |
| | | | | | | | | | | | | | | | | | | | | | | | | | 8 | | | | | |
| | | | | | | | | | | | | | | | | | | | | | | | | | 9 | | | | | |
| | | | | | | | | | | | | | | | | | | | | | | | | | 10 | | | | | |
| | | | | | | | | | | | | | | | | | | | | | | | | | 11 | | | | | |
| | | | | | | | | | | | | | | | | | | | | | | | | | 12 | | | | | |
| | | | | | | | | | | | | | | | | | | | | | | | | | 13 | | | | | |
| | | | | | | | | | | | | | | | | | | | | | | | | | 14 | | | | | |
| | | | | | | | | | | | | | | | | | | | | | | | | | 15 | | | | | |
| | | | | | | | | | | | | | | | | | | | | | | | | | 16 | | | | | |
| | | | | | | | | | | | | | | | | | | | | | | | | | 17 | | | | | |
| | | | | | | | | | | | | | | | | | | | | | | | | | 18 | | | | | |
| | | | | | | | | | | | | | | | | | | | | | | | | | 19 | | | | | |
| | | | | | | | | | | | | | | | | | | | | | | | | | 20 | | | | | |
| | | | | | | | | | | | | | | | | | | | | | | | | | 21 | | | | | |
| | | | | | | | | | | | | | | | | | | | | | | | | | 22 | | | | | |
| | | | | | | | | | | | | | | | | | | | | | | | | | 23 | | | | | |
| | | | | | | | | | | | | | | | | | | | | | | | | | 24 | | | | | |
| | | | | | | | | | | | | | | | | | | | | | | | | | 25 | | | | | |
| | | | | | | | | | | | | | | | | | | | | | | | | | 26 | | | | | |
| | | | | | | | | | | | | | | | | | | | | | | | | | 27 | | | | | |
| | | | | | | | | | | | | | | | | | | | | | | | | | 28 | | | | | |
| | | | | | | | | | | | | | | | | | | | | | | | | | 29 | | | | | |
| | | | | | | | | | | | | | | | | | | | | | | | | | 30 | | | | | |
| | | | | | | | | | | | | | | | | | | | | | | | | | 31 | | | | | |
| | | | | | | | | | | | | | | | | | | | | | | | | | 32 | | | | | |
| | | | | | | | | | | | | | | | | | | | | | | | | | 33 | | | | | |
| | | | | | | | | | | | | | | | | | | | | | | | | | 34 | | | | | |
| | | | | | | | | | | | | | | | | | | | | | | | | | 35 | | | | | |
| | | | | | | | | | | | | | | | | | | | | | | | | | 36 | | | | | |

# Notes

# Daily Lesson Plans Section

# Week of _____

| Subject or Section | MONDAY | TUESDAY | WEDNESDAY |
|---|---|---|---|
| Period | | | |
| Period | | | |
| Period | | | |
| Period | | | |
| Period | | | |
| Period | | | |
| Period | | | |

*Absence makes the heart grow fonder.*

| THURSDAY | FRIDAY | NOTES: |
|---|---|---|
| | | |

# Week of _____

| Subject or Section | MONDAY | TUESDAY | WEDNESDAY |
|---|---|---|---|
| Period | | | |
| Period | | | |
| Period | | | |
| Period | | | |
| Period | | | |
| Period | | | |
| Period | | | |

*From little acorns mighty oaks do grow.*

| THURSDAY | FRIDAY | NOTES: |
|----------|--------|--------|
|          |        |        |

# Week of _____

| Subject or Section | MONDAY | TUESDAY | WEDNESDAY |
|---|---|---|---|
| Period | | | |
| Period | | | |
| Period | | | |
| Period | | | |
| Period | | | |
| Period | | | |
| Period | | | |

*Actions speak louder than words.*

| THURSDAY | FRIDAY | NOTES: |
|---|---|---|
|  |  |  |

# Week of _____

| Subject or Section | MONDAY | TUESDAY | WEDNESDAY |
|---|---|---|---|
| Period | | | |
| Period | | | |
| Period | | | |
| Period | | | |
| Period | | | |
| Period | | | |
| Period | | | |

*All that glitters is not gold.*

| THURSDAY | FRIDAY | NOTES: |
|---|---|---|
|  |  |  |

# Week of _____

| Subject or Section | MONDAY | TUESDAY | WEDNESDAY |
|---|---|---|---|
| Period | | | |
| Period | | | |
| Period | | | |
| Period | | | |
| Period | | | |
| Period | | | |
| Period | | | |

*April showers bring May flowers.*

| THURSDAY | FRIDAY | NOTES: |
|---|---|---|
| | | |
| | | |
| | | |
| | | |
| | | |
| | | |
| | | |

# Week of _____

| Subject or Section | MONDAY | TUESDAY | WEDNESDAY |
|---|---|---|---|
| Period | | | |
| Period | | | |
| Period | | | |
| Period | | | |
| Period | | | |
| Period | | | |
| Period | | | |

*Beauty is only skin deep.*

| THURSDAY | FRIDAY | NOTES: |
|---|---|---|
|  |  |  |

# Week of _____

| Subject or Section | MONDAY | TUESDAY | WEDNESDAY |
|---|---|---|---|
| Period | | | |
| Period | | | |
| Period | | | |
| Period | | | |
| Period | | | |
| Period | | | |
| Period | | | |

*Don't put the cart before the horse.*

| THURSDAY | FRIDAY | NOTES: |
|----------|--------|--------|
|          |        |        |
|          |        |        |
|          |        |        |
|          |        |        |
|          |        |        |
|          |        |        |
|          |        |        |

# Week of _____

| Subject or Section | MONDAY | TUESDAY | WEDNESDAY |
|---|---|---|---|
| Period | | | |
| Period | | | |
| Period | | | |
| Period | | | |
| Period | | | |
| Period | | | |
| Period | | | |

*Don't count your chickens before they hatch.*

| THURSDAY | FRIDAY | NOTES: |
|---|---|---|
| | | |

# Week of _____

| Subject or Section | MONDAY | TUESDAY | WEDNESDAY |
|---|---|---|---|
| Period | | | |
| Period | | | |
| Period | | | |
| Period | | | |
| Period | | | |
| Period | | | |
| Period | | | |

*Don't cry over spilt milk.*

| THURSDAY | FRIDAY | NOTES: |
|----------|--------|--------|
|          |        |        |
|          |        |        |
|          |        |        |
|          |        |        |
|          |        |        |
|          |        |        |
|          |        |        |

# Week of _____

| Subject or Section | MONDAY | TUESDAY | WEDNESDAY |
|---|---|---|---|
| Period | | | |
| Period | | | |
| Period | | | |
| Period | | | |
| Period | | | |
| Period | | | |
| Period | | | |

*The early bird catches the worm.*

| THURSDAY | FRIDAY | NOTES: |
|---|---|---|
|  |  |  |

# Week of _____

| Subject or Section | MONDAY | TUESDAY | WEDNESDAY |
|---|---|---|---|
| Period | | | |
| Period | | | |
| Period | | | |
| Period | | | |
| Period | | | |
| Period | | | |
| Period | | | |

*Honey catches more flies than vinegar.*

| THURSDAY | FRIDAY | NOTES: |
|---|---|---|
|  |  |  |
|  |  |  |
|  |  |  |
|  |  |  |
|  |  |  |
|  |  |  |
|  |  |  |

# Week of _____

| Subject or Section | MONDAY | TUESDAY | WEDNESDAY |
|---|---|---|---|
| Period | | | |
| Period | | | |
| Period | | | |
| Period | | | |
| Period | | | |
| Period | | | |
| Period | | | |

*A friend in need is a friend indeed.*

| THURSDAY | FRIDAY | NOTES: |
|---|---|---|
| | | |

# Week of _____

| Subject or Section | MONDAY | TUESDAY | WEDNESDAY |
|---|---|---|---|
| Period | | | |
| Period | | | |
| Period | | | |
| Period | | | |
| Period | | | |
| Period | | | |
| Period | | | |

*Genius is 1% inspiration and 99% perspiration.*

| THURSDAY | FRIDAY | NOTES: |
|---|---|---|
| | | |
| | | |
| | | |
| | | |
| | | |
| | | |
| | | |

# Week of _____

| Subject or Section | MONDAY | TUESDAY | WEDNESDAY |
|---|---|---|---|
| Period | | | |
| Period | | | |
| Period | | | |
| Period | | | |
| Period | | | |
| Period | | | |
| Period | | | |

*The grass is always greener on the other side of the fence.*

| THURSDAY | FRIDAY | NOTES: |
|---|---|---|
| | | |

# Week of _____

| Subject or Section | MONDAY | TUESDAY | WEDNESDAY |
|---|---|---|---|
| Period | | | |
| Period | | | |
| Period | | | |
| Period | | | |
| Period | | | |
| Period | | | |
| Period | | | |

*Haste makes waste.*

| THURSDAY | FRIDAY | NOTES: |
|---|---|---|
| | | |

# Week of _____

| Subject or Section | MONDAY | TUESDAY | WEDNESDAY |
|---|---|---|---|
| Period | | | |
| Period | | | |
| Period | | | |
| Period | | | |
| Period | | | |
| Period | | | |
| Period | | | |

*Here today, gone tomorrow.*

| THURSDAY | FRIDAY | NOTES: |
|---|---|---|
|  |  |  |

# Week of _____

| Subject or Section | MONDAY | TUESDAY | WEDNESDAY |
|---|---|---|---|
| Period | | | |
| Period | | | |
| Period | | | |
| Period | | | |
| Period | | | |
| Period | | | |
| Period | | | |

*Hitch your wagon to a star.*

| THURSDAY | FRIDAY | NOTES: |
|---|---|---|
|  |  |  |

# Week of _____

| Subject or Section | MONDAY | TUESDAY | WEDNESDAY |
|---|---|---|---|
| Period | | | |
| Period | | | |
| Period | | | |
| Period | | | |
| Period | | | |
| Period | | | |
| Period | | | |

*Imitation is the sincerest form of flattery.*

| THURSDAY | FRIDAY | NOTES: |
|---|---|---|
| | | |
| | | |
| | | |
| | | |
| | | |
| | | |
| | | |

# Week of _____

| Subject or Section | MONDAY | TUESDAY | WEDNESDAY |
|---|---|---|---|
| Period | | | |
| Period | | | |
| Period | | | |
| Period | | | |
| Period | | | |
| Period | | | |
| Period | | | |

*Knowledge is power.*

| THURSDAY | FRIDAY | NOTES: |
|---|---|---|
| | | |

# Week of _____

| Subject or Section | MONDAY | TUESDAY | WEDNESDAY |
|---|---|---|---|
| Period | | | |
| Period | | | |
| Period | | | |
| Period | | | |
| Period | | | |
| Period | | | |
| Period | | | |

*Look before you leap.*

| THURSDAY | FRIDAY | NOTES: |
|---|---|---|
|  |  |  |
|  |  |  |
|  |  |  |
|  |  |  |
|  |  |  |
|  |  |  |
|  |  |  |

# Week of _____

| Subject or Section | MONDAY | TUESDAY | WEDNESDAY |
|---|---|---|---|
| Period | | | |
| Period | | | |
| Period | | | |
| Period | | | |
| Period | | | |
| Period | | | |
| Period | | | |

*Love makes the world go around.*

| THURSDAY | FRIDAY | NOTES: |
|---|---|---|
|  |  |  |

# Week of _____

| Subject or Section | MONDAY | TUESDAY | WEDNESDAY |
|---|---|---|---|
| Period | | | |
| Period | | | |
| Period | | | |
| Period | | | |
| Period | | | |
| Period | | | |
| Period | | | |

*Make haste slowly.*

| THURSDAY | FRIDAY | NOTES: |
|---|---|---|
|  |  |  |

# Week of _____

| Subject or Section | MONDAY | TUESDAY | WEDNESDAY |
|---|---|---|---|
| Period | | | |
| Period | | | |
| Period | | | |
| Period | | | |
| Period | | | |
| Period | | | |
| Period | | | |

*Make hay while the sun shines.*

| THURSDAY | FRIDAY | NOTES: |
|---|---|---|
|  |  |  |
|  |  |  |
|  |  |  |
|  |  |  |
|  |  |  |
|  |  |  |
|  |  |  |

# Week of _____

| Subject or Section | MONDAY | TUESDAY | WEDNESDAY |
|---|---|---|---|
| Period | | | |
| Period | | | |
| Period | | | |
| Period | | | |
| Period | | | |
| Period | | | |
| Period | | | |

*Many hands make light work.*

| THURSDAY | FRIDAY | NOTES: |
|---|---|---|
|  |  |  |
|  |  |  |
|  |  |  |
|  |  |  |
|  |  |  |
|  |  |  |
|  |  |  |

# Week of _____

| Subject or Section | MONDAY | TUESDAY | WEDNESDAY |
|---|---|---|---|
| Period | | | |
| Period | | | |
| Period | | | |
| Period | | | |
| Period | | | |
| Period | | | |
| Period | | | |

*Never put off until tomorrow what you can do today.*

| THURSDAY | FRIDAY | NOTES: |
|---|---|---|
|  |  |  |
|  |  |  |
|  |  |  |
|  |  |  |
|  |  |  |
|  |  |  |
|  |  |  |

# Week of _____

| Subject or Section | MONDAY | TUESDAY | WEDNESDAY |
|---|---|---|---|
| Period | | | |
| Period | | | |
| Period | | | |
| Period | | | |
| Period | | | |
| Period | | | |
| Period | | | |

*Nothing succeeds like success.*

| THURSDAY | FRIDAY | NOTES: |
|---|---|---|
| | | |

# Week of _____

| Subject or Section | MONDAY | TUESDAY | WEDNESDAY |
|---|---|---|---|
| Period | | | |
| Period | | | |
| Period | | | |
| Period | | | |
| Period | | | |
| Period | | | |
| Period | | | |

*One picture is worth a thousand words.*

| THURSDAY | FRIDAY | NOTES: |
|---|---|---|
|  |  |  |
|  |  |  |
|  |  |  |
|  |  |  |
|  |  |  |
|  |  |  |
|  |  |  |

# Week of _____

| Subject or Section | MONDAY | TUESDAY | WEDNESDAY |
|---|---|---|---|
| Period | | | |
| Period | | | |
| Period | | | |
| Period | | | |
| Period | | | |
| Period | | | |
| Period | | | |

*One rotten apple spoils the barrel.*

| THURSDAY | FRIDAY | NOTES: |
|---|---|---|
|  |  |  |
|  |  |  |
|  |  |  |
|  |  |  |
|  |  |  |
|  |  |  |
|  |  |  |

# Week of _____

| Subject or Section | MONDAY | TUESDAY | WEDNESDAY |
|---|---|---|---|
| Period | | | |
| Period | | | |
| Period | | | |
| Period | | | |
| Period | | | |
| Period | | | |
| Period | | | |

*The pen is mightier than the sword.*

| THURSDAY | FRIDAY | NOTES: |
|---|---|---|
|  |  |  |

# Week of _____

| Subject or Section | MONDAY | TUESDAY | WEDNESDAY |
|---|---|---|---|
| Period | | | |
| Period | | | |
| Period | | | |
| Period | | | |
| Period | | | |
| Period | | | |
| Period | | | |

*A penny saved is a penny earned.*

| THURSDAY | FRIDAY | NOTES: |
|---|---|---|
|  |  |  |

# Week of _____

| Subject or Section | MONDAY | TUESDAY | WEDNESDAY |
|---|---|---|---|
| Period | | | |
| Period | | | |
| Period | | | |
| Period | | | |
| Period | | | |
| Period | | | |
| Period | | | |

*Practice makes perfect.*

| THURSDAY | FRIDAY | NOTES: |
|---|---|---|
| | | |

# Week of _____

| Subject or Section | MONDAY | TUESDAY | WEDNESDAY |
|---|---|---|---|
| Period | | | |
| Period | | | |
| Period | | | |
| Period | | | |
| Period | | | |
| Period | | | |
| Period | | | |

*Rome wasn't built in a day.*

| THURSDAY | FRIDAY | NOTES: |
|---|---|---|
|  |  |  |

# Week of _____

| Subject or Section | MONDAY | TUESDAY | WEDNESDAY |
|---|---|---|---|
| Period | | | |
| Period | | | |
| Period | | | |
| Period | | | |
| Period | | | |
| Period | | | |
| Period | | | |

*Silence is golden.*

| THURSDAY | FRIDAY | NOTES: |
|---|---|---|
|  |  |  |

# Week of _____

| Subject or Section | MONDAY | TUESDAY | WEDNESDAY |
|---|---|---|---|
| Period | | | |
| Period | | | |
| Period | | | |
| Period | | | |
| Period | | | |
| Period | | | |
| Period | | | |

*A stitch in time saves nine.*

| THURSDAY | FRIDAY | NOTES: |
|---|---|---|
|  |  |  |
|  |  |  |
|  |  |  |
|  |  |  |
|  |  |  |
|  |  |  |
|  |  |  |

# Week of _____

| Subject or Section | MONDAY | TUESDAY | WEDNESDAY |
|---|---|---|---|
| Period | | | |
| Period | | | |
| Period | | | |
| Period | | | |
| Period | | | |
| Period | | | |
| Period | | | |

*Don't throw out the baby with the bath water.*

| THURSDAY | FRIDAY | NOTES: |
|---|---|---|
|  |  |  |
|  |  |  |
|  |  |  |
|  |  |  |
|  |  |  |
|  |  |  |
|  |  |  |

# Week of _____

| Subject or Section | MONDAY | TUESDAY | WEDNESDAY |
|---|---|---|---|
| Period | | | |
| Period | | | |
| Period | | | |
| Period | | | |
| Period | | | |
| Period | | | |
| Period | | | |

*Truth will out.*

| THURSDAY | FRIDAY | NOTES: |
|---|---|---|
|  |  |  |

# Week of _____

| Subject or Section | MONDAY | TUESDAY | WEDNESDAY |
|---|---|---|---|
| Period | | | |
| Period | | | |
| Period | | | |
| Period | | | |
| Period | | | |
| Period | | | |
| Period | | | |

*A watched pot never boils.*

| THURSDAY | FRIDAY | NOTES: |
|---|---|---|
|  |  |  |
|  |  |  |
|  |  |  |
|  |  |  |
|  |  |  |
|  |  |  |
|  |  |  |

# Week of _____

| Subject or Section | MONDAY | TUESDAY | WEDNESDAY |
|---|---|---|---|
| Period | | | |
| Period | | | |
| Period | | | |
| Period | | | |
| Period | | | |
| Period | | | |
| Period | | | |

*Where there's a will, there's a way.*

| THURSDAY | FRIDAY | NOTES: |
|---|---|---|
| | | |

# Week of _____

| Subject or Section | MONDAY | TUESDAY | WEDNESDAY |
|---|---|---|---|
| Period | | | |
| Period | | | |
| Period | | | |
| Period | | | |
| Period | | | |
| Period | | | |
| Period | | | |

*A word to the wise is sufficient.*

| THURSDAY | FRIDAY | NOTES: |
|---|---|---|
| | | |

# Week of _____

| Subject or Section | MONDAY | TUESDAY | WEDNESDAY |
|---|---|---|---|
| Period | | | |
| Period | | | |
| Period | | | |
| Period | | | |
| Period | | | |
| Period | | | |
| Period | | | |

*If the shoe fits, wear it.*

| THURSDAY | FRIDAY | NOTES: |
|---|---|---|
|  |  |  |

# Week of _____

| Subject or Section | MONDAY | TUESDAY | WEDNESDAY |
|---|---|---|---|
| Period | | | |
| Period | | | |
| Period | | | |
| Period | | | |
| Period | | | |
| Period | | | |
| Period | | | |

*Hunger is the best pickle.*

| THURSDAY | FRIDAY | NOTES: |
|---|---|---|
|  |  |  |

# Notes